Securing Women's Economic Security, Safety, and Freedom

Universal basic income (UBI) as a policy measure for supporting economic security has attracted worldwide attention. This book contributes to the discussion by focusing on UBI's potential impacts for women, including women of colour and First Nations women.

Utilizing a "scenario interviewing" approach, the author worked with 26 diverse Australian women to imagine the potential implications of UBI for their own lives, as well as for women more broadly. The women talked about a range of possible impacts including poverty reduction, economic security, improved autonomy, and freedom from violence, which are sorted into overarching themes and chapters. Integrating these women's narratives into the key arguments for and against UBI, this book provides a robust and readable introduction to relevant literature.

This book is suitable for a wide audience including scholars and students across the social sciences, as well as policymakers.

Zoe Staines is a senior lecturer and researcher at The University of Queensland, School of Social Science. Her research and qualifications, including PhD, span social policy, gender and work, critical criminology, and intersectionality. Her professional experiences extend across academia, government, and the non-profit sector.

Securing Women's Economic Security, Safety, and Freedom

The Role of Universal Basic Income in Australia

Zoe Staines

Routledge
Taylor & Francis Group
LONDON AND NEW YORK

First published 2025
by Routledge
4 Park Square, Milton Park, Abingdon, Oxon OX14 4RN

and by Routledge
605 Third Avenue, New York, NY 10158

Routledge is an imprint of the Taylor & Francis Group, an informa business

British Library Cataloguing-in-Publication Data
A catalogue record for this book is available from the British Library

ISBN: 9781032957876 (hbk)
ISBN: 9781032957906 (pbk)
ISBN: 9781003586593 (ebk)

DOI: 10.4324/9781003586593

Typeset in Galliard
by KnowledgeWorks Global Ltd.

Contents

Acknowledgements

This book was written on the sovereign, unceded lands of the Yagera and Turrbal peoples in Meanjin (Brisbane), the Kombumerii peoples in Jellurgal (Burleigh Heads), and the Quandamooka peoples on Jencoomercha (Macleay Island, Moreton Bay), Australia. My deepest acknowledgment and respect goes to Elders past and present, who continue to care for and nurture these lands and seas, as well as be cared for and nurtured by them in return.

Thank you to the Whitlam Institute, including Director Professor John Jurianz, for the opportunity to conduct the research project that provided the foundation for this book. Thanks to Dr Andrea Connor for the provocations, guidance, and support you provided along the way. And thanks also to Professor Azadeh Dastyari for your warm support during the final stages of the project, as well as the encouragement to turn my project findings into this book. The excellent work that the Whitlam Institute continues to do in celebrating the many legacies of former Prime Minister Gough Whitlam, as well as the incredible record of his government's short-lived leadership of Australia, is truly admirable. I am humbled to have been able to contribute in some small way.

My deepest thanks to the esteemed colleagues who reviewed the research report that formed the basis for this book: Emeritus Professor Marian Sawer AO FASSA (Australian National University), Professor Almaz Zelleke (New York University, Shanghai), and Associate Professor Ben Spies-Butcher (Macquarie University). I have deep respect and admiration for your work and am truly grateful that you took the time to provide such valuable feedback on mine. Of course, any omissions and errors in this book are solely my own.

A big thank you to my most excellent Research Assistant, Ms Barbara Wood, who helped with refining the interview protocol and conducting some of the interviews for this research. Thank you also to my other wonderful Research Assistant, Ms Mel Powersmith, who helped with undertaking literature searches to inform aspects of this report. You'll both go far.

To my darling daughter, I hope one day you'll live in a fairer Australia where the sex you were assigned at birth, or the gender you choose for yourself, does not determine your economic security and safety. I love you with all my heart; I know you'll grow up to be fierce and brave in everything you do. To my dearest and most beautiful mum, had your own biological mother been able to receive independent economic support to care for you as a single parent, I wonder whether she would have still made the agonising decision to give you up for adoption. Finally, to my dear partner, Greg, thank you for always reminding me that there is far more to life than work.

1 Introduction

> I think, for women … [UBI] would dramatically improve the conditions of their lives… if women had that bit more … control or autonomy over their own lives, perhaps the world wouldn't get away with the way that it treats women.
>
> (Casey, 47 years)

Over recent decades, the nature of work, social organisation, and daily life has undergone significant and rapid change. Amongst these shifts, paid work has become more precarious and a far weaker source of economic security. At the same time, states have tended to withdraw social supports in the name of austerity, including by diminishing social housing stocks, lowering income benefits, and tightening eligibility for these (and other) economic safety nets. These transformations have been further compounded by global crises, such as pandemics and climate change, which continue to bring into sharper relief longer-standing fractures in our modes of economic organising that distribute the burdens and benefits of paid and unpaid work unevenly across populations. This was particularly apparent during the COVID-19 pandemic, where renewed attention was directed towards women's disproportionate responsibility for caregiving, and the way that this inflected not only their economic (in)security but also their risk of falling ill—particularly as frontline workers across typically feminised professions (nursing, teaching, childcare, aged care). However, this is not new.

In 2018, before COVID-19 took hold, women across the globe performed about 76.5% of all total hours of unpaid care work, while "In no country in the world do men and women provide an equal share" (ILO, 2018, p. 37). By 2020, women worldwide spent about three times as many hours as men on unpaid domestic work and care: approximately 4.2 versus 1.7 hours per day (United Nations, 2020). Even though these gaps are already enormous, they grow even wider when we consider how they are also modulated by other aspects of social identity, including race,

DOI: 10.4324/9781003586593-1

class, ability, and more. For instance, the time First Nations women across Australia spend doing unpaid care work is huge: approximately double that of non-Indigenous Australian women (Hunter et al., 2016; Klein et al., 2024; Yap & Biddle, 2012). This is also echoed in other parts of the world and is informed by long histories of oppression, including violent exploitation under (setter) colonial expansion (e.g., Anishinaabe et al., 2022; McKinley et al., 2021). Within this context, prioritising care and other unpaid work can also be a critical act of resistance against the hegemony of (white) "Western" capitalism (Klein et al., 2024). Nevertheless, this means that women overall are less likely to participate in the formal economy, juggling multiple expectations of work, family, and more by either reducing their paid work hours, staying in lower-paid positions with greater flexibility, and/or stepping away from paid work altogether. In 2023, women's worldwide labour force participation was a mere 48.7% compared with 73.1% for men, leaving a difference of 24.5% (World Bank, 2023).[1] This contributes to a persistent global gender pay gap, which saw women earning only about 68.4% of men's average incomes in 2023 (World Economic Forum, 2024). In 2024, the World Economic Forum's "Global Gender Gap Index"—which considers not only economic participation and opportunity, but also educational attainment, health, and political empowerment—was estimated at 31.5% (68.5% closed) across the 146 included nations.

These circumstances raise important and pressing questions about the best strategies for securing women's economic security, safety, and freedoms into the future. Typically, public policy responses to such questions are refracted through a liberal feminist lens, prioritising the perceived need for human capital investment in women to lift their labour force participation, while also improving their representation in higher-paid sectors and positions (Rottenberg, 2022). This is exemplified in continued calls to "shatter the glass ceilings" that prevent women's advancement in paid work (e.g., Champoux-Paillé & Croteau, 2023; Meyerson & Fletcher, 2000). At its core, however, this approach undervalues the care and other work that women (but also, all genders) do—often beyond the remit of the formal economy—and perpetuates the (artificial) prioritisation of paid work over all other forms of productivity and relational labour: a phenomenon that has only arisen relatively recently, since the European Industrial Revolution. Ironically, it does this while at the same time consistently making demands for paid workers to achieve a "better work-life balance" (Champoux-Paillé & Croteau, 2023). The responsibility for achieving this elusive balance is typically shifted back onto the worker themselves, regularly with very little or no attention given to how institutional structures make this near impossible for many, particularly women, and especially women also experiencing other intersectional disadvantages (e.g., see Shattell, 2017). Meanwhile, under this approach, the above-mentioned gaps in labour force representation, income, and gender equality between men and women *are* closing, but at an agonisingly slow rate.

At the current pace,[2] the gap in labour-force participation between men and women will not close until around the year 2232—207 years from now, while it will take until the year 2129 for the global gender pay gap to also close—104 years from now (author's own calculations, based on World Economic Forum data [World Economic Forum, 2023]).[3] Similarly, the World Economic Forum (2024) reports that at the current rate of progress, it will take 134 years to reach full parity against the Global Gender Gap Index. Worryingly, these are *optimistic* estimates that do not consider worst-case scenarios for those experiencing multiple marginalisation, and/or the impacts of global pandemics and natural disasters, which are predicted to occur at escalating rates and have been shown to at least pause, if not reverse, progress towards parity. In the meantime, the economy continues to "free ride" on women's unpaid work (Fraser, 2016), while women themselves overwhelmingly experience economic insecurity, as well as the myriad negative flow-on effects that accompany it. It is against this backdrop that a relatively old idea and the core topic of this book—universal basic income (UBI)—has garnered new and growing attention.

What is known about a UBI for women?

The historical roots of UBI are disputed (Sloman et al., 2019), though some have suggested it dates as far back as the ancient Athenians (~460s BC) (Standing, 2015). Whatever its origin,[4] UBI is underpinned by the concept of distributing common resources in a way that upholds a basic standard of living for all. Or as Bidadanure (2019, p. 82) puts it, "a commitment to the view that a share of the wealth produced by all in common, or by previous generations, should be redistributed to all in the form of a direct payment to individuals". UBI is defined by the Basic Income Earth Network (BIEN, 2023) as "a periodic cash payment unconditionally delivered to all on an individual basis, without means-test or work requirement". The BIEN General Assembly has, moreover, affirmed that a UBI should be "stable in size and frequency and high enough to be, in combination with other services, part of a policy strategy to eliminate material poverty and enable the social and cultural participation of every individual" (Yamamori 2016 in Henderson, 2019, p. 255). This relates to Van Parijs' (1997, 2004) theorising of UBI as a simple way of achieving "real freedom". That is, being free to do what one wishes, as well as having the means to do so.

UBI has continued to grow in popularity, entering mainstream public and political discourse in many parts of the world. Proposals and pilots have also arisen worldwide, with existing research highlighting myriad benefits including the removal of punitive conditions attached to welfare receipt, reductions in poverty rates, and the pursuit of ecological sustainability/post-productivism (e.g., Büchs, 2021; Standing, 2017; Widerquist, 2018). However, even though scholarly attention around UBI has recently increased, most existing literature does not delve deeply into possible gendered impacts. For instance, across the 44 most popular social science academic databases and only considering outputs published in the decade from 2013 to 2023, the Boolean search phrase "basic income" returns 8,356 results, while '"basic income" + women' returns just 210 (~2.5%). Of these, only 78 make any significant mention of gendered impacts (i.e., more than a simple mention in passing), and just 18 report empirical research results, rather than only theorising about the impacts of UBI. Nevertheless, across this relatively small group of existing studies, some common themes arise.

First, UBI is regularly positioned as a means of improving women's economic security (e.g., Alstott, 2001; Cameron & Tedds, 2021; Davala et al., 2015; Kowalska, 2023; Lapine et al., 2021; Pin et al., 2023). Indeed, there is good evidence that UBI and similar programs can successfully reduce poverty, including for women from diverse backgrounds (de Souza, 2021; Levasseur et al., 2018; Onifade et al., 2023). Trials of UBI in India, for instance, have been especially beneficial for improving the economic position of women, as well as those in lower castes and those who live with disabilities (Davala et al., 2015, 2017). Meanwhile, in Mississippi (United States), a UBI pilot that pays $12,000 USD per annum ($1k per month) from the Magnolia Mothers' Trust to 110 Black single mothers has shown significant impacts around not only poverty, but also health, well-being, and social connectedness (Luterman, 2022; Onifade et al., 2023). This is not to suggest, however, that the poverty-reduction effects of UBI are universally agreed (Chrisp, 2023).

In Peru and Indonesia there is evidence that targeted assistance measures are more effective at reducing poverty than UBI, since incomes are not documented for large parts of the population, thereby affecting the ability of the state to tax back UBI payments from those with higher incomes (Hanna & Olken, 2018). Overall, UBI would thus reduce the per capita amount able to be provided and be less efficient in directing resources to those most in need (Hanna & Olken, 2018; also see Piachaud, 2018). In a similar vein, Greenstein (2019) argues that conservative approaches to UBI that see it as a blanket replacement for social security have the potential to *increase*, rather than reduce, poverty. This is because programs (including cash transfers) currently targeted to those in poverty would be removed and the funding used to support those programs effectively redistributed upward to all, regardless of income (though this does not account for the recouping of costs from those with higher incomes via taxation).

Notwithstanding these complexities, and since a key driver of women's economic insecurity across the globe is the continued devaluing of their unpaid reproductive labour, an important potential impact of UBI lies in its ability to make the choice to undertake these and other diverse forms of labour less financially detrimental (e.g., Alstott, 2001; Chung, 2023; Kowalska, 2023; Lapine et al., 2021; Morini, 2021). Indeed, UBI may—as found in Canada under a 2015 basic income pilot ($16,989 per year, less 50% of earnings)—enable family units to make different decisions around the distribution of paid work and unpaid childcare, potentially freeing up women's time where there is an additional adult in the household (Hamilton, 2020; Pin et al., 2023). In contrast, however, some feminist scholars argue that since UBI remains contextually situated within late capitalism, it has potential to further perpetuate rather than overcome oppressive gendered power relations that are inherent within capitalism (e.g., Gheaus, 2008; Göker, 2018; Miller et al., 2023; Thompson, 2022; Weeks, 2011; Zelleke, 2008, 2011). That is, UBI may further entrench unequal gender roles by incentivising women *away* from the labour force while continuing to render their reproductive labour comparatively less valuable in monetary terms, since a UBI is unlikely to ever match the economic benefits of wage labour (including wage growth, superannuation, paid leave, etc.) (Roebyns, 2000; Widerquist, 2018). This concern is borne out in findings from a recent macro-simulation model, based on Italian time-use data, which shows that even though a "care income" would improve women's total income, both a "care income" *and* UBI tend to direct women out of the labour force and thus reduce their receipt of other wage labour benefits (Cieplinski et al., 2023; also see Bibler et al., 2023). Similarly, in a recent scoping review, which drew on evidence from 27 separate studies of nine policy interventions similar to UBI (i.e., negative income tax, resource rents, and unconditional transfers), Gibson et al. (2020) found that women with younger children tended to respond by reducing their hours of paid employment, choosing instead to spend more time providing unpaid care. The fact, however, that findings across these studies are mixed suggests that outcomes will differ according to context.

In Australia, a 2021 survey (*N*=1,001) canvassing how the general public would react to the introduction of a permanent UBI showed that exactly the same proportion of women and men (12%) indicated that they would reduce their paid work hours, while the proportions of men responding that they would take on additional parenting responsibilities (12%) and additional domestic/household responsibilities (15%) were higher than for women (9% and 12%, respectively) (Anglicare Australia,

2021). This suggests a possible (albeit slight) redistributive effect, though these are intentions only that may change in practice. In Colombia, Pfutze and Rodríguez-Castelán (2019) showed that unconditional payments of 41,000 Colombian Pesos per month (around $15.70 AUD) to women aged 52+ years and men aged 57+ years resulted in people *increasing* their overall participation in the workforce by eliminating financial barriers to such participation. This was especially the case for men, though there was still a weaker effect for women, while other women already in paid work also shifted from lower- to higher-paid positions. Similarly, the aforementioned study of UBI for 110 Black mothers in Mississippi (United States) found that, when compared with a control group of 40 mothers who did not receive the UBI, there was no discernible change in workforce participation (Onifade et al., 2023).

Ultimately, these mixed findings suggest that women's diversion away from employment is not an inevitable outcome of UBI, and nor is it necessarily an undesirable one. Indeed, at the very least, UBI can potentially create conditions where all genders are freed up to make different decisions about how they distribute and share unpaid labour, thereby providing a mechanism for pursuing what Fraser (1997, p. 61) refers to as a "universal caregiver" model, which aims to make "women's current life-patterns the norm for everyone" (see also Zelleke, 2008). This is set in opposition to simply achieving "care parity" whereby a care income, UBI, or similar might make up for (some) income inequalities but do nothing to redistribute the work of caregiving more equally across genders, and/or a "universal breadwinner" model, whereby parity in employment is prioritised instead and supported through the provision of commodified forms of care (Fraser, 1997). Indeed, and as Zelleke (2011, p. 33) argues, a UBI:

> ...may lead to a society in which ... gender differences do not penalise women (or men) who choose not to pursue androcentric ideals of citizenship by relegating them to poverty, dependence on their spouses or employers, and second-class citizenship.

However, what is clear is that, perhaps unsurprisingly, a UBI alone cannot correct deeply entrenched gender inequalities that animate patriarchal capitalism in the first place, and which continue to perpetuate women's economic insecurity as well as men's "caring insecurity" (Cook, 2019, p. 198; also see Yamashita, 2017). Indeed, significant social and cultural shifts, including shifts in other major social institutions (e.g., education, work, housing, social security), are needed if gendered norms around the (re)distribution of paid and unpaid work are to change in ways that improve circumstances and outcomes for women over the long term (Hester & Srnicek, 2023; Koslowski & Duvander, 2018; Lombardozzi, 2020), and in ways that might bring societies closer to realising Fraser's (1997) "universal caregiver" objective to truly "live differently" (Ketterer, 2021; Zelleke, 2011).

Another key theme across existing studies on UBI and women concerns its role in supporting women's more general empowerment and freedom (e.g., Howard, 2015; Morini, 2021). For instance, analysing historical survey data from the 1974–1979 Canadian "Mincome" (Manitoba Basic Annual Income Experiment), Gonalons-Pons and Calnitsky (2022) found that it helped dilute the effects of "male breadwinner" policies, providing women with an independent source of income that improved their bargaining power in personal relationships (also see Katada [2014] in relation to Japan). Ultimately, this improved the ability of women to exercise voice and exit, including from relationships where violence was present (also see Grey, 2019; Kawagoe, 2019). Jauch (2015) similarly reports that a basic income guarantee ("BIG") trial in Namibia not only reduced poverty and improved well-being but also supported women's financial independence, reducing their economic reliance on men and reducing participation in (sometimes violent) sex work (also see Makole et al., 2022; Miller et al., 2023 in relation to Bangladesh). Morini (2021) sees this empowerment effect as a key benefit of UBI for women, improving their self-determination and emancipating them from the existential uncertainty generated by reliance on men (Cameron & Tedds, 2021; Gil, 1981), and/or on incomes generated via precarious employment or social security (also Miller et al., 2023). In this regard, Enríquez (2016, p. 43) describes UBI as having the potential to function like an "emancipation allowance", improving women's "bargaining power vis-à-vis their employers *and* spouses" (emphasis added).

These (and other) arguments continue to animate and characterise international debates about the potential impacts of UBI for women and beyond. As indicated earlier, however, they are heavily dependent on the context within which UBI is experienced, as well as being reliant on how a UBI is designed. As Enríquez (2016) contends, myriad outcomes from UBI are possible, but these depend on several interwoven factors, such as:

> i) the monetary level of [U]BI vis-à-vis the level of wages; ii) labour market opportunities, available (or not) for men and women; iii) labour conditions in feminized economic sectors; iv) the existence and efficiency of public policies to confront gender discrimination in the labour market; v) cultural values concerning gender roles in productive and reproductive work spheres; [and] vi) the availability of accessible care services.

Regarding Enríquez's (2016) first point alone, proposals and trials of UBI worldwide have tested diverse payment rates and arrangements, with per month rates ranging significantly, from $35 USD/$47 AUD (Brazilian Citizen's Basic Income) to $500 USD/$671 AUD (Stockton California trial), to $635 USD/$852 AUD (Finland), to $1,430 USD/$1,920 AUD (Germany), or to $1,968 USD/$2,643 AUD (Spain) (Samuel 2020). Ultimately, Miller et al. (2023, p. 192) state simply that "The larger the Basic Income, the larger would be the gender egalitarian effects", arguing that it should be set at least at a rate that enables "a foundation of economic security" for those who need to rely on it while undertaking unpaid work such as care. Nevertheless, this variability reinforces the need for further studies that not only have a more dedicated focus on how UBI might produce gendered impacts but also take geopolitical context *and* UBI design seriously. This book represents an attempt to do this, exploring the possible effects of a UBI for diverse women within the specific geopolitical context of Australia.

UBI for women: Australia as a case study

Although Australia has not yet experienced a national UBI pilot, a small-scale basic income trial run between 1972 and 1975 by non-profit organisation, the Brotherhood of St Laurence, showed excellent potential (Brotherhood of St Laurence, 2017; Gilley, 1991). The trial engaged 60 low-income Melbourne families in family support and provided them with an unconditional income supplement. Women involved in the project spoke about the importance of having an income paid directly to them rather than their partners—a measure that strongly supported their autonomy and independence (Gilley, 1991). In addition to this small trial, Australia's federal Commission of Inquiry into Poverty, led by Professor Ronald Henderson ("the Henderson Inquiry"), also recommended in 1975 a national UBI-like scheme. However, as I elaborate on in Chapter 2, this was never taken up. In the decades since, discussions around the possibilities of a UBI have grown more frequent, particularly since 2016, with the publication of a research paper concerning UBI in the Australian Parliamentary Library (Arthur, 2016). Subsequent Australian studies concerning UBI have canvassed (at least):

- different justifications for UBI (e.g., Klein et al., 2019; Mays & Marston, 2016),
- political strategy (e.g., Barrett, 2017; Henderson, 2021; Luccioni, 2020; Marston & Peterie, 2020; Patulny & Spies-Butcher, 2023; Spies-Butcher et al., 2023),
- econometric modelling (e.g., Phillips, 2018),

- media framings (e.g., Carroll & Engel, 2021),
- potential impacts (e.g., Anglicare Australia, 2021; Cox, 2019; Morley et al., 2019), and
- possible policy approaches that would see a categorical UBI introduced for specific groups, such as First Nations peoples or mothers (e.g., Bueskens, 2017; Fouksman & Klein, 2019; Goreng-Goreng [Wakka Wakka], 2017; Krakouer [Mineng Noongar], 2020).

In addition to growing research attention around UBI in Australia, COVID-19 changes to Australian social security during 2020, which were akin to a targeted and categorical UBI, gave helpful insight into the possible poverty-reduction effects of this policy in practice (ACOSS, 2022). These changes, which removed conditionality from a raft of existing social security payments, and dramatically increased the level of such payments, resulted in a 17-year low poverty rate after nearly 20 years of little movement at all (ACOSS, 2022). This drastically (though temporarily) improved the lives of thousands of the most marginalised Australians, including thousands of women, their dependents, and communities (Klein et al., 2022a, 2022b; Staines & Zahnow, 2022).

While UBI is far from universally supported in Australia (e.g., Cowan, 2017), survey research has indicated that there is a growing proportion of the population who *do* support it (Biddle et al., 2022; Hollo, 2020; Patulny & Spies-Butcher, 2023). For instance, in a panel survey run between May 2019 and February 2020, Patulny and Spies-Butcher (2023) found that 51% of Australians supported the policy. By October 2020, support had reached 58% (The Green Institute, 2020) before increasing sharply in May 2021 during the height of Australia's COVID-19 experience to 77% (Azize, 2021) and then falling back to 55% in October of the same year (Biddle et al., 2022). A more recent survey, which I ran in November 2024 with a nationally representative weighted sample of 2,000 Australians, indicated that support has remained stable and relatively high, sitting at 59.5% (Staines, 2025). These relatively high levels of support, however, belie the fact that realising a UBI for Australia remains a significant challenge with several crucial barriers remaining, including cost, funding avenues, design, and ideological opposition to what some see as UBI's threat to the paid work ethic. Ultimately, when considering UBI for Australia, many also warn that it is not a panacea and that eliminating poverty, including for women, requires multiple strategies (Henderson, 2019; Klein et al., 2021). Henderson (2019, p. 259) argues, for example, "we must adopt a pragmatic approach regarding the prioritisation of [basic income] versus, say, increasing disability support payments and services, or childcare support". Others have proposed that coupling a UBI with a public-sector job guarantee may provide a more effective policy for reducing poverty while also tackling under/unemployment

(Fitzroy & Jin, 2018), particularly in areas like remote Australia, where unemployment is structural and persistent (Staines, 2022).

Overall, additional intersectional work is needed to explore not only the gendered effects of an Australian UBI, but also those that are inflected by race, class, ability, and more (McLean, 2016; Miller et al., 2023). Considering how these might play out in the specific geopolitical context of Australia is important and, as noted earlier, is a key reason for the focus of this book. Indeed, as a settler colony, Australia has built its contemporary nationhood on the oppression of First Nations peoples. Notwithstanding similarities with other settler colonies, including Canada and Aotearoa (New Zealand), this provides a particular and somewhat unique backdrop for considering the potential of UBI for women, within which First Nations women are multiply oppressed and undertake the largest amounts of unpaid work in the country (Klein et al., 2024; Moreton-Robinson, 2000). This context also raises important questions about strategies for funding a UBI. For instance, First Nation peoples' never ceded sovereignty over Australian lands and seas renders funding approaches like those adopted in Alaska, where revenues from the nation's natural oil reserves are distributed as an annual citizen dividend, potentially unviable and unethical in relation to a national Australian UBI—or at least one that is inclusive of settlers. Moreover, the Australian case study holds important lessons in terms of understanding how multiple and interwoven policies and regulations can modify the potential impacts of UBI for women. In this sense, considering UBI *within* the Australian context enables a "ground truthing" of existing literature that still overwhelmingly theorises about UBI, rather than drawing deeply on contextualised empirical accounts. Many of the lessons that arise from the empirical exploration described in the chapters of this book are, nevertheless, highly relevant to other international jurisdictions, particularly those with similar policy architectures and settler-colonial histories (e.g., the United Kingdom, the United States of America, Canada, Aotearoa/New Zealand, and many European nations).

Aims and approach of this book

In this book, I grapple with several key international debates around the gendered effects of UBI, anchoring them through the stories and experiences of 26 women who live across six of Australia's eight total states and territories. These stories derive from a series of interviews, undertaken in 2023–2024 for a study I completed into UBI in Australia. I undertook this study during an appointment as Whitlam Research Fellow with the Western Sydney University's Whitlam Institute—a research and policy think tank established in honour of the memory and work of former Australian Labor Prime Minister, Gough Whitlam AC QC. Women were recruited to the study via a mixture of social media callouts and "snowballing", whereby existing contacts led to the identification of further possible participants. Overall, the approach to selecting women was "purposive" in nature, insofar as the intention was to recruit women to the study who had a diverse range of backgrounds and experiences. Notwithstanding some limitations (which I outline later), this was successful, with the 26 participants including women from their late teens to those in their late 60s; those who identify as First Nations, migrant, and non-migrant; some of whom are engaged with Australia's social security system and others who aren't; those who live in urban and non-urban settings; those with and without employment, disability, and more.

Women's stories were captured via a "scenario interviewing" approach, where they were presented with a UBI scenario for Australia and invited to imagine the potential implications of this for them, as well as for Australian women more broadly. All interviews were undertaken between July and October 2023 by myself and research assistant, Ms. Barbara Wood. We asked women to focus on possible impacts around poverty reduction, economic security, autonomy, and freedom, though other topics and themes also arose organically. The UBI scenario was the same for all women, involving a government-provided, taxable UBI set at $1,203 AUD per fortnight ($31,278 AUD per year)—which was equivalent to Australia's "Henderson poverty line" for a single person at the time of data collection (March quarter, 2023—see Melbourne Institute, 2023a).

As discussed earlier, there is considerable variation in the levels of UBI proposed and/or piloted across the globe. The amount adopted for this study is, for example, slightly less than the proposed two-year UK trial of ~$1,516 AUD (£800) per fortnight (Ali Hussen, 2023), and slightly more than the Irish trial (from September 2022 to 2025) of ~$1,060 AUD (€650) per fortnight for artists (see Irish Government, 2022). In relation to Australia, this amount also sits at roughly the level set in the 2022 proposal by The Greens for a Liveable Income Guarantee (i.e., $88 AUD per day or $1,232 AUD per fortnight) (The Greens, 2022) and is slightly more than the amount proposed in the 2020 Liveable Income Guarantee (participation income) proposal by a group of Australian scholars (Quiggin et al., 2020a, 2020b), which used Australia's age pension as a benchmark (i.e., $944.30 AUD per fortnight at that time, or $1,047.10 AUD per fortnight using the updated 2024 rate). Nevertheless, in keeping with the focus of this study on improving women's economic security, safety, and freedom, and in line with the reasoning of others around the need for a UBI to enable poverty reduction, Australia's "Henderson poverty line" was chosen as the most suitable benchmark for the UBI scenario in this study. For further details about the specific methods used in this research, please see Appendix 1.

At the outset of the interviews, and prior to describing the amount settled upon for the scenario provided to the women participants, we first asked women what amount of UBI per fortnight might be "meaningful to them". The responses varied (min=$600 AUD per fortnight, max=$4,300 AUD per fortnight), though the average across all respondents was $1,550 AUD per fortnight: only slightly higher than the scenario amount of $1,203. In relation to this, there was also overwhelming agreement across the interviewees that some groups would still, regardless of the existence of a UBI, require additional top-ups whether in the form of additional categorical payments, and/or quality services:

> It needs to still be acknowledged that programs like that, need to support the additional things that come with being disabled... It can't be that the basic income just covers everything, because it ... couldn't.
>
> (Hannah, 42 years)

Overall, most of the women we spoke to had at least a general idea of what UBI was, having heard or read about it in recent news and other media. The characteristics of UBI that were most salient for the women we spoke to were that it is:

- universal (that is, "distributed to every person" [Holly, 27 years]; "[given] to all citizens" [Camille, 42 years]; "every citizen of a country or locale" [Terri, 30 years]),
- non-means and non-activity tested (e.g., "regardless of wealth or circumstances" [Holly, 27 years]; "obligation free" [Fiona, 60 years]; "unconditional...support" [Shania, 31 years]), and
- designed to cover basic needs (e.g., "a base rate pay" [Tracy, 46 years]; "so you can survive" [Layla, 20 years]; "an amount that would cover basic bills and living expenses" [Hannah, 42 years]).

At the outset of the interviews, prior to any other lines of questioning that might have influenced their responses, we asked women whether they were in favour of or against UBI. Most, though not all, of the women we spoke to were in favour of a UBI for Australia overall. Some tempered their support by also talking about what they saw as possible negative impacts, including possible economic inflation (Zayla, 31 years), and questions around universality, particularly whether those already well off deserve to receive it (Marley, 35 years; Pat, 52 years). However, overwhelmingly, women saw UBI as having potentially positive impacts, as I canvass throughout the book.

Ultimately, the stories told by the women in this book offer glimpses into the complexities of their lives, including frustrations with the economic insecurities thrust upon them by systems that are not designed *by* or *for* them, struggles with violence (both past and present), the challenges of juggling paid and unpaid work, and more. Across these stories there are elements of pain, despair, and frustration, but also of strength, resilience, hope, and gratitude. I have sorted these stories and experiences into key overarching themes, which I have translated into an overall structure for the book.

While the next chapter (Chapter 2) sets further context for understanding these women's stories by summarising the demographic, historical, and geopolitical milieu of Australia, Chapter 3 critically discusses women's views and concerns about how UBI might influence their experiences of economic (in)security. In this chapter, women speak to social expectations around their labour, as well as the structural disadvantages they face that worsen their economic insecurity. While they consider the ways in which UBI might assist, they also talk about how it does not go far enough; deeper and longer-lasting changes to social norms and institutions are also needed to improve women's economic security into the future. This relates to the themes explored in Chapter 4, which covers the potential impact of UBI in tackling violence against women. In this chapter, I show how violence—in myriad forms—was a core topic across all of the women's stories, whether they spoke about themselves as victims and/or their close female family, kin, friends, colleagues, and others. While, again, UBI may provide a partial response, far more needs to be done to address the social and cultural determinants of this violence, including the ways it is entrenched within and perpetuated by major social institutions (the economy, the social security system, and more).

Chapter 5 discusses women's views about UBI in relation to their health and well-being. Many of the women in this study identified as living with one or more disabilities and thus, managing and improving their health and well-being became a central point of concern in the stories they told. For some, a UBI would help support access to fundamental facilities that were unavailable via existing government programs. In many other cases, women spoke of the sheer relief and "wiggle room" that a UBI might provide, which would allow them to "breathe again", while also affording to take more proactive care of their health and well-being by eating well, having regular medical check-ups, exercising, and being able to cover needed medical devices and supports. In all cases, UBI was viewed as a potential means of assisting women to improve their health as well as that of their children (where applicable) and, in some cases, to recover after long periods of illness. Importantly, women also spoke about how, in addition to a UBI, Australia's healthcare system needs to be overhauled, again drawing attention to the need for complementary policies and programs, rather than considering UBI as a standalone intervention. Finally, Chapter 6 draws out some overarching conclusions about the possible impacts of UBI for women in Australia. It discusses policy and research implications both within the Australian context, and beyond.

Ultimately, the question this book sets out to answer was most eloquently articulated by one of the women interviewees themselves—Casey (47 years). Casey is a mother, low-income earner, social security recipient, and lives with multiple disabilities. She grew up in a violent household and also experienced violence as an adult, at the hands of a (now former) partner. Casey asked, simply: if a UBI were introduced, would the world "get away with the way that it treats women"? Casey's experiences, but also her hope that UBI might give greater "autonomy and control" to women, reflect the strength and optimism that come through in not only her own story, but also in many other women's stories that are woven through this book. To Casey, and to all of the 26 women who shared their stories with me and Barbara, we offer our deepest gratitude. Thank you for trusting us enough to share these glimpses into your lives. It is my hope that, at the very least, this book will contribute to answering Casey's question. At best, it might also help to inform, in some small way, a different future for women: one where economic security, safety, and "real freedom" are firm realities for all.

Notes

1 This also varies considerably across national contexts. For the latest comparisons, see: https://genderdata.worldbank.org/en/indicator/sl-tlf-acti-zs

2 That is, approximately −0.11675 on average per year, based on change between 1991 and 2023 (author's calculations based on World Bank, 2023).

3 This applies to the rate of change in the global gender pay gap between 2022 and 2023: that is, 0.3 percentage points per year (World Economic Forum, 2023).

4 The genealogy of UBI is not the focus of this book, and there are many other editions available for this purpose (e.g., Sloman et al., 2019; Standing, 2015; Widerquist, 2024).

2 Putting UBI into context

> I see the benefit [of UBI] to Australian women being great... We know that there is the gender pay gap. We know that there is unequal care. Even just basic things around how ... this [might] influence parental leave and how people might approach raising their families when there is that less pressure around "Where is the next pay cheque coming from?"
>
> (Kiah, 39 years)

This chapter seeks to "set the scene" for the remainder of this book by doing two things. First, it introduces Australia as a case study, detailing its settler-colonial context, demographic profile, geopolitical milieu, and changing approach to social assistance. This includes key social policy changes affecting women across the 20th and 21st centuries, with more recent shifts occurring within a period of neoliberal paternalism (Soss et al., 2011), whereby eligibility for social security has been tightened and conditionalities intensified. These measures have been justified by a "politics of blame" that casts those seeking social security assistance as morally corrupt and as a burden upon taxpayers (Saunders, 2019, p. 19). Considering this longer history, including impacts for women, provides a helpful backdrop for deliberations around UBI as an alternative policy approach today. It is also important for "grounding" women's narratives, which appear across subsequent chapters.

Second, this chapter outlines past and present Australian policy proposals for UBI (and similar) as well as key arguments that animate them. This includes, for instance, a small 1970s UBI pilot run by a non-profit, a proposal for a UBI-like policy arising from a 1970s Royal Commission into Poverty, and more recent proposals presented by political parties, independents, and scholars that canvass at least partially categorical or targeted UBIs for women, mothers, First Nations peoples, and more. Ultimately, this chapter demonstrates, in a fuller way, that context matters greatly in discussions about UBI. In providing this more detailed context, the chapter foregrounds and anchors the themes and stories that arise in

DOI: 10.4324/9781003586593-2

subsequent chapters. In many respects, the stories and accounts that appear in the remainder of the book cannot be understood separately to the detailed context laid out here.

Setting the scene: the Australian context

Australia is often erroneously referred to as a "young" or "new" country, having only been federated in 1901 after its violent colonisation by British (and non-British) convicts and free settlers from 1788 (Chingaipe, 2024; Moreton-Robinson, 2015). In reality, archaeological evidence indicates that occupation of the lands now referred to as Australia stretch much further back to at least 65,000 years ago (Clarkson et al., 2017), with Aboriginal and Torres Strait Islander Dreaming stories articulating even deeper, ongoing connections to Country, as well as associated "creativity, imagery, and intuition" (Poelina et al., 2023). Of course, continued discursive references to Australia's relative "youth" are not unintentional; they form part of historic and continuing settler-colonial efforts to erase the continent's rich pre-colonial history, which runs anathema to British occupiers' insistence that the lands of Australia were previously uninhabited under the legal doctrine of *terra nullius*. The overturning of this legal doctrine under *Mabo v. Queensland (No 2)* in 1992 officially uncovered the reality of invasion and theft of Aboriginal and Torres Strait Islander lands by non-Indigenous colonisers, though nation-wide truth-telling about the genocidal violence that characterised this theft is continuing to unravel, albeit excruciatingly slowly (Davis, 2022; Wolfe, 2006). This includes unearthing continuing forms of colonial violence, such as systemic and interpersonal racism, whose symptoms generate devastating social outcomes, while ensuring that—to the country's great shame—Aboriginal and Torres Strait Islander peoples in Australia are the most incarcerated peoples on the planet (Anthony, 2017; Davis, 2022; Dudgeon & Walker, 2022). First Nations women are Australia's fastest growing prison population, with socioeconomic insecurities as well as direct and intergenerational traumas being regular features of inmates' histories, layered upon the traumas of imprisonment itself (Fryer, 2024; Howard-Wagner & Brown, 2021; Kendall et al., 2020). It is against this backdrop that contemporary Australian identity, politics, and policy are formed.

In early 2025, Australia's total population was just over 27.5 million (ABS, 2025a) with 3.3% of the population identifying as Aboriginal and/or Torres Strait Islander—a minority that is continuing to grow despite the devastation of colonialism (ABS, 2021a). At the most recent 2021 Census, the median age for all Australians was 38 years, with 50.7% identifying as female and 49.3% as male (ABS, 2021a). (Controversially, at the time of writing, the ABS continues not to release data on non-binary sex or gender identities [ABS, 2022].) Less than half (46.5%) of all Australians aged 15+ years were married at the time of the 2021 Census, with 36.5% having never been married, 8.8% having divorced, and 3.2% having been separated (ABS, 2021a). Notwithstanding the country's settler colonial foundations and abhorrent record on asylum seeker policy (e.g., Amnesty International, 2016), the Australian Government (n.d., p. 7) describes it as "the most successful multicultural society in the world", with 33.1% of Australians having been born overseas (ABS, 2021a) and a further 48.2% having at least one parent born overseas (ABS, 2021a).

In January 2025, Australia's seasonally adjusted unemployment rate was 4.1% (representing about ~615,100 unemployed persons total), while its underemployment rate was 6.0% (ABS, 2025b). Youth unemployment sat at 9.0%, with the overall labour force participation rate (that is, all people either employed or looking for work) being 67.3% (ABS, 2025b). As in other parts of the world, Australian women are less likely than men to participate in the labour force (63.5% of women compared to 71.3% of men) and are more likely to be underemployed (7.1% of women versus 5.0% of men) (ABS, 2025b). Aboriginal and Torres Strait Islander women are nearly 10% less likely to be in the labour force than non-Indigenous women and are also more likely to be unemployed (ABS, 2021b). Over time, Australia has experimented with different forms of social assistance, including cash transfers, to support those who find themselves unemployed, as well as other groups requiring support. I turn to some points on this timeline below.

Australian social assistance: shifting sands

Prior to federation of Australia in 1901, poverty assistance was largely the purview of charities (Marston & Staines, 2019; Smyth, 2012). After federation, however, the foundations of a national welfare state began to take shape (Marston & Staines, 2019; Smyth, 2012). The first minimum "living wage" was established for Australian workers under the Harvester Judgement, handed down by Justice Higgins of the Court of Conciliation and Arbitration in 1907 (Marston & Staines, 2019). Soon, in 1908, the Australian government introduced a fixed-rate age pension, though it was means tested and some groups, including Aboriginal and Torres Strait Islander peoples, were excluded altogether, being classified at the time as non-citizens (Marston & Staines, 2019).

After WWII, the Australian welfare state grew exponentially with the aim of improving postwar life (Shaver, 1987). This resulted in the creation of what Castles (1985) has referred to as a "wage-earner's welfare state"—or a *white, male* wage-earner's welfare state as Bryson (1992) later pointed out. This was reflected in the design, for instance, of key federal social security payments directed specifically towards women during the early part of the 20th century,[1] which primarily aimed to support them and their children from destitution upon loss of a male breadwinner's wage (Cook, 2019; Herscovitch & Stanton 2008; O'Neill & Johns 2009; Reid, 2023; ; Smith, 2017). Meanwhile, unmarried mothers were nearly entirely unsupported, meaning "The only real option for many women who were single and pregnant was to relinquish their baby for adoption" (Edwards, 2023, p. 170). For Aboriginal and Torres Strait Islander peoples, who were not recognised as Australian citizens until 1949 (Jordens, 1999),[2] eligibility for social security was not available at all until a 1959 amendment to the *Social Services Act* (Cth) (Marston & Staines, 2020). Even then, strict requirements around documentation still effectively excluded many individuals from claiming until much later, and it was not until 1966 that restrictions on the receipt of social security payments by Aboriginal and Torres Strait Islander peoples were lifted altogether (Marston & Staines, 2020). This preceded the 1967 Australian Referendum, which saw the Australian government able to make laws concerning Aboriginal and Torres Strait Islander peoples for the first time.

The 1950s–1960s represented a period of relative stagnation for Australia's welfare state, with strong employment during this time (Regan, 2014). However, this changed dramatically with the election of a new Labor Government under Prime Minister Gough Whitlam in 1972, and the advent of a global recession in 1974, prompting a period of rapid social policy reform. Whitlam was an innovator, being unafraid to experiment with significant shifts in social policy (Peachment, 1976). He sought to give the Commonwealth a lead role in social welfare provision (Coleman, 2023), and his emphasis on poverty reduction led his government to prioritise the needs of those most at risk, particularly women and First Nations peoples. On matters relating to both groups, Whitlam made significant progress.[3] With regard to women in particular, the Whitlam Government enacted wide-reaching reforms, appointing the first-ever adviser on women's affairs in Elizabeth Reid (later, Dr Elizabeth Reid), introducing no-fault divorce, ushering in the Country's first-ever Supporting Mother's Benefit, and much more (Arrow, 2023). Many of these policies emanated from the influence of the Australian feminist movement of the 1960s and 1970s; particularly from the Women's Liberation Movement (WLM) and from the associated Women's Electoral Lobby (WEL) (Arrow, 2023; Reid, 2023). This included the WEL's strong Aboriginal and Torres Strait Islander members, such as Pat Eatock, who fought for intersectional justice (Eatock, 1986; Eatock & Eatock, 2023). The Council of Single Mothers and their Children (CSMC), formed in Melbourne in 1969, also strongly agitated for improved support for sole mothers (Edwards, 2023).[4]

Whitlam's sweeping changes were underpinned by a strong conviction that women's inequality was rooted in patriarchal mistruths that maintained their subjugation. For instance, on his announcement of the momentous Royal Commission on Human Relationships (1974), which had broad terms of reference and powers enabling it to inquire into myriad social issues facing women, Whitlam (in Reid, 2023, p. 15) explained:

> Before we can act in this area, we must know why all this is so and what can be done to change it... The cause lies invariably in the deeply ingrained cultural assumptions that every woman's primary role is that of daughter, wife, mother, mother-in-law, or grandmother; nurse, secretary, teacher, or shop assistant; the deeply ingrained assumption that women are here to serve or assist. The wellbeing of men and children within our society must not be at the expense of the wellbeing of their wives and mothers. For this is too high a price to pay.

Whitlam's public demands to address patriarchal norms and values, and to elevate the place of women in Australian society, were translated into action via a suite of policy interventions that dramatically changed Australian women's lives,[5] including cash transfers directly aimed at women, albeit with a primary focus on women as carers (Cook, 2019). By way of example, the *Maternity Leave Act 1973 (Cth)* enabled women working in the public service to receive 12 weeks of full pay and 12 months of unpaid leave to care for their children (Reid, 2023). The Supporting Mother's Benefit, also implemented in 1973, represented another significant and momentous reform that changed many women's lives.

The Supporting Mother's Benefit was paid to sole mothers following a six-month waiting period.[6] By aiming to assist women sole parents to be able to raise their children *regardless* of the presence of a male breadwinner, the Benefit rubbed against dominant cultural mores that denigrated unmarried and single mothers, labelling their children as "bastards" or worse (Coleman, 2023; Edwards, 2023; McDonald & Spindler, 1988; Young, 2012). In an historical review of the changing position of the father under Australian child custody law, for instance, James (2006) explained that:

> A "fatherless" child was [understood in law as] a bastard, then illegitimate and then ex-nuptial; while the mother was a harlot or strumpet, then a fallen woman, an unmarried mother and later a single mother. There appears to be no discriminatory language for the man involved who, until the innovation of DNA testing in the mid-1980s, was only the "putative father" because while motherhood was a matter of fact, fatherhood was a matter of opinion.

Within this context, and as Edwards (2023, p. 169) described it, the Supporting Mother's Benefit effectively meant that "eliminating State-sanctioned harm for single mothers and their children was achieved in less than 18 months". As Reid (2023, p. 25) explained:

> This measure gave women a sense of agency, increased their self-esteem and provided financial independence. It changed our language—no longer were such children [of these single mothers] stigmatically classified as "illegitimate" or "bastards" and it moved a whole group of women out of poverty and despair.

It also marked a shift in social security provision towards viewing women as independent beneficiaries, though in ways that were still contingent on their acting as primary carers (Cook, 2019)—similar to a "care income" (Cieplinski et al., 2023). Nevertheless, this helped to prevent single mothers from falling into poverty and dramatically reduced the previously high adoption rates for children born out of wedlock and/or without a second parent figure (Edwards, 2023; Howe & Swain, 1993; Young, 2012).

The payment rate for the Supporting Mother's Benefit was set at the level for Commonwealth Class A widows, being ~$36 per week in 1973 and rising to $118 per week by 1985, initially sitting higher than rates for other Commonwealth benefits and pensions (e.g., Classes B/C widows, age pension, and unemployment benefits) (McDonald & Spindler, 1988). This was also higher than the national Child Endowment rate (initially five shillings or ~50c per week). Moreover, the benefit was simple and straightforwardly administered via the (then) Department of Social Security and, until 1986–1987, a claim could be lodged "entirely by mail", with a decision about whether a non-essential interview should take place being left to the discretion of local Departmental officers (McDonald & Spindler, 1988, p. 4).

Take up of the Supporting Mother's Benefit was rapid; by 1974, 26,286 Australian women were receiving it, ~54% of whom were unmarried (McDonald & Spindler, 1988; Reid, 2023, p. 25). In 1977, the Benefit was extended to single fathers, being renamed the Supporting Parents Benefit, though it was disproportionately women who continued to receive it (Cook, 2019). By June 1986, 176,730 sole parents were subscribed, with the overall outlay reaching $1.3 billion by 1988 (McDonald & Spindler, 1988).

The payment had considerable impacts for Australian women, with Reid (2023, p. 25) describing the benefit as "Perhaps the policy that most challenged and changed the structural underpinnings of patriarchy". In summarising the possible impacts of the policy, McDonald & Spindler (1988, p. 6) suggested that it could affect:

> ...the decision [of a second parent] to pay maintenance if separated; the decision of a husband or wife to remain in a de jure or de facto

marriage; the decision of a woman to become pregnant or, if pregnant, to abort, give up for adoption or keep the child; the decision of (actual or potential) sole parents to work full-time, part-time or not at all, or to work in the "cash" or illegal economy or, if not working, to be counted as unemployed or as a pensioner; and, the choice of location, accommodation, consumption and investment goods.

At the Whitlam Institute's launch of Dr Elizabeth Reid's legacy report (Reid, 2023) in Canberra on 28 September 2023, women in attendance spoke to me about the numerous benefits that the Supporting Mothers/Parents Benefit had for them personally, as well as their friends and family. One woman recalled that a single mother friend declared to her that it was due to the Supporting Mother's Benefit that she could afford, for the first time, to eat regular food, rather than surviving on dog food—her only affordable option prior to receiving the payment. This story, and others like it, demonstrate the important gains that can be made when policies support women's independent economic security. Nevertheless, notwithstanding this win for a gender-sensitive policy approach under Whitlam, neoliberalism soon began to seep into Australia's social welfare state almost in lock step with the rise of the Australian WLM and associated increased demands on state support. This has had myriad significant impacts for social security policy, and in turn, the economic security of Australian women.

In the 50 or so years since the Whitlam Government and Henderson Inquiry, and particularly since the late 1980s, neoliberalism has increasingly imbued Australian social policy, resulting in (and often enforcing) free-market expansion while prioritising individual independence from the state (Harvey, 2007; Soss, et al. 2011). As Sawer (in Arrow, 2023, p. 7) described it, "just as the State was becoming more responsive to the diverse needs of women [during the early 1970s], this other [neoliberal] revolution was taking place, lowering expectations of the State as a source of social justice". By the early 21st century, "the post-Henderson era of women's entitlement based on care-related 'difference' was coming to an end" (Cook, 2019, p. 191).

From the late 1970s onwards, "A 'business case' now had to be presented to justify gender equality policies" (Sawer, 2023, p. 7), as the economic "bottom line" became a key marker by which policy interventions were assessed, achieved by either cutting or recouping welfare costs. Meanwhile, neoliberal imaginaries of so-called "welfare dependency" have become increasingly deeply embedded in popular discourse, labelling and stigmatising those in receipt of social security cash transfers—and particularly single mothers, First Nations women, and women of colour—as "lazy", "bludgers", "drug-addicted", "poor decision makers", and worse (Marston et al., 2022; O'Connor, 2001; Saunders, 2019). This has produced considerable harm for social security recipients subjected to these damaging narratives (e.g., Marston et al., 2022; Staines et al. 2021b). Overall, Saunders (2019, pp. 19–20) describes Australia's current social security system as one that takes a:

> …"tough love" approach characterised by the absurd slogan that "the best form of welfare is a job" and an unending drive to tighten eligibility conditions (conditionality) and erode payment adequacy, invisibly through flawed indexation arrangements… The idea that the social security system is a fundamentally cohesive and empowering public institution designed to meet the needs of all Australians has been replaced by a divisive politics of blame which sees "them"—the victims of economic and social change—cast as a burden on "us" taxpayers. [Moreover] Welfare reform has become a vehicle for devising new ways of coercing the unemployed and jobless into jobs that are increasingly insecure and poorly paid, providing no guarantee against in-work poverty, but making the alternatives increasingly unpalatable.

Currently, Australia's public social expenditure (i.e., expenditure by governments at all levels on social assistance and insurance payments) amounts to approximately 20.5% of the country's total gross domestic product (GDP) (OECD, 2024). Compared with other countries in the Organization for Economic Cooperation and Development (OECD), this places it 18th out of 37, and just above the overall OECD average of 20.1% of GDP (OECD, 2024) (see Appendix 1). Over time, this expenditure as a proportion of GDP has increased (see Appendix 2), though this has occurred while eligibility for social security payments and obligations attached to them has been tightened.

At the end of 2024, women represent ~67% of total recipients for the core social security payment types outlined in Table 2.1 (and across all Australian payment types, they represent 64% of total recipients) (DSS, 2024). This means they are both more likely to be subjected to punitive conditionalities, and more likely to have their economic insecurity worsened by low payment rates. For instance, the base rates for the allowance and pension types in Table 2.1 sit between 43% and 86% of the Henderson Poverty Line. Moreover, benefits have overwhelmingly become contingent on workforce participation for women, with payments aimed at supporting caregiving having been eroded, and women (and indeed, all people) now being viewed as "workers first and carers second" (Cook, 2019, p. 191). To support this aim, government policy now strongly focuses on subsidising commodified forms of care, such as paid childcare, so that caregivers (still predominantly women) can spend more time in wage labour—a trend I discuss further in Chapter 3 (Brennan, 2019; Cook, 2019).

Table 2.1 Selected characteristics of core Australian social security payment types

Selected payment types	*Proportion recipients who are female (%)*	*Base payment rate (per week)*	*Base payment rate as proportion (%) of Henderson Poverty Line (for single person)*
Parenting payment (single)	94%	$503.75 (single)	82%[a]
Parenting payment (partnered)	90%	$356.15 (partnered)	43%[b]
Carer payment	71%	$523.55 (single)	86%[a]
Age pension	56%	$523.55 (single)	86%[a]
Disability support pension	47%	$523.55 (single)	86%[a]
JobSeeker payment	46%	$389.00 (single, no children)	64%[a]
	Average[c] = 67%		

Notes: Recipient details are based on DSS data extracted in September 2024. Base payment rates are based on Services Australia data, in September 2024. Henderson Poverty Line rate is based on reporting from the June quarter, 2024 (latest available at the time of writing). [a]Based on Henderson Poverty Line for a single adult person (head in workforce)—$612.18 per week. [b]Based on Henderson Poverty Line for an adult couple (head in workforce)—$818.92 per week. [c]An average rather than overall total proportion is presented here because payment categories are not mutually exclusive (i.e., an individual can be a recipient across multiple categories).

Returning to the Supporting Mothers/Parents Benefit described earlier, eligibility began to be more strictly monitored via periodic compulsory interviews and reports, a reduction in child age requirements for eligibility,[7] and the preclusion of co-residing, from 1986/1987 onwards (Cook, 2019; McDonald & Spindler, 1988). McDonald and Spindler (1988, p. 4) explained that the intention of these changes was, apparently, to ensure that "entitlement be correctly established rather than restricted, although the latter might be an unintended consequence". This statement is an eery read in 2025, where Parenting Payments (the contemporary equivalent of the Supporting Mothers/Parents Benefit) are now arguably more difficult than ever to access, with tightened eligibility and with a very recent history of incredibly harmful conditions (Cook, 2019; Murphy, 2024). As Coleman (2023, p. 127) reflected, the system of support for sole parents was essentially "destroyed" under the Howard Liberal/National Coalition Government (1996–2007), which saw parents forced onto unemployment benefits and associated "mutual obligation" programs when their youngest child turned eight years of age. The subsequent Gillard Labor Government "completed this destruction, moving the 'grandfathered' women onto unemployment payments"

(Coleman, 2023, p. 127). In practice, this had the effect of withdrawing benefits from approximately 150,000 single Australian mothers on the same day as Julia Gillard—Australia's first (and at the time of writing, only) female Prime Minister—made her historic "misogyny speech" in the Australian Parliament, calling out the sexism of her fellow parliamentarians (Bueskens, 2019).[8] Meanwhile, unemployment mutual obligation programs have ushered in very high rates of breaching and associated losses of social security income, especially in remote First Nations communities, often producing significant poverty (e.g., Staines, 2022; Staines et al., 2021a).

Later, from 2018, Australia's experimentation with the ParentsNext Program further intensified mutual obligations for unemployed parents of children aged between six months and eight years (if single) or six years (if partnered) (Hamer & Tranter, 2021). As part of the Program's "activation" requirements, Parenting Payment recipients (around 96% of whom remained women) had to engage with private employment service providers to undertake training and upskilling activities or were otherwise subject to targeted compliance measures, including payment suspensions and withdrawals (Hamer & Tranter, 2021). This affected the basic rights of Australian women to enjoy equal access to income support (Goldblatt, 2022) and further exacerbated their poverty, especially for single mothers (Cook, 2019; Klein, 2021a). As Klein (2021a) also documented, ParentsNext completely missed the value of caregiving, perpetuating the patriarchal notion that this is entirely separate from the economy (rather than *underpinning* it) and less important than wage labour. Klein (2021b) argues, therefore, that the program represented a new era in the continued expropriation of women's labour which, for First Nations women, was layered upon long-standing patterns of colonial expropriation. In response to the recommendations of a 2019 Senate inquiry, ParentsNext became voluntary in May 2023 and ended on 31 October 2024, being replaced by a new voluntary program, "Parent Pathways", aimed to "help parents with young children... meet [their] personal, study, or work goals" (Services Australia, 2024c, 2024d). Although this was considered a "win" by many (e.g., Council of Single Mothers and their Children, 2023), the "work-first" approach nevertheless continues. Ultimately, as Cook (2019, p. 192) describes it, this approach "that treats low-income mothers as male breadwinners fails to account for women's lived reality or social policy needs" (Cook, 2019, p. 192). Moreover, the entrenchment of what Cook (2019) refers to as a "gender regime" in Australian social policy means that, even if women and men choose to undertake the opposite sex's gendered roles "(childless women managers or stay-at-home dads), ... the roles themselves remain unchanged" (Probert in Cook, 2019, p. 194).

Alongside the intensive targeting of parents through workforce activation policies, Australia's couple rule—which classifies partnered social security recipients as a single financial unit—also persists and continues to disproportionately affect women (Sleep, 2023). As Sleep (2023) and others have argued, this rule fails to appreciate power dynamics that impact the distribution of income across household members: a particular issue for women experiencing domestic and family violence, as I expand on in Chapter 4. Moreover, Australia's current social security and taxation systems continue to combine to produce considerable inefficiencies, such as very high effective marginal tax rates (EMTRs), which effectively penalise individuals for earning higher incomes by combining income taxes with social security benefit withdrawals. This creates poverty traps, especially for those in precarious, casual, and part-time jobs—most often women (Ingles et al., 2019). Overall, and as Cook (2019, p. 197) reflects:

> ... women's poverty and men's hampered ability to provide care are embedded within [Australian social] policy and reveal that despite significant policy reform and women's entry into work, little has changed in terms of the underlying gender roles... This is far from the ideals proposed by Henderson regarding a form of basic income [the Guaranteed Minimum Income or GMI] that could free up both men and women to more easily combine work and care.

Ultimately, although the Whitlam era saw considerable expansion of social security rights for Australian women, these have largely contracted since the late 1970s. When situated within this longer history, the Whitlam Government's reform legacy appears even more profound, offering a glimpse into an alternative means of addressing poverty and economic insecurity in Australia. In the meantime, public attention around the need to reduce poverty—particularly for women remains consistently strong (Saunders, 2019). Conversely, the path towards achieving this goal remains unclear. It is within this broader context that deliberations around a UBI for Australia have continued. This extends previous historical considerations of an Australian UBI, which I turn to below.

Australia and a UBI: A missed opportunity in 1975?

Attention around a UBI in Australia has fluctuated over time. As mentioned in Chapter 1, the nation has only experienced one small UBI pilot, conducted by non-profit, the Brotherhood of St Laurence, between 1972 and 1975. The pilot was more akin to a categorical basic income (rather than full UBI), as it targeted 60 low-income Melbourne families (Brotherhood of St Laurence 2017; Gilley, 1991). Aside from this, and notwithstanding a diversity of current UBI proposals, the Henderson Inquiry's 1975 proposal of a Guaranteed Minimum Income (GMI) is widely acknowledged to have been another serious contender. Indeed, Henderson's GMI represented somewhat of a "sliding doors" moment for Australia, coming immediately prior to the steering of Australian policy towards a strong neoliberal path, described earlier.

Following research into poverty by Henderson and colleagues in the late 1960s, and amidst Whitlam's lobbying for an inquiry into poverty during his time as opposition leader, the Henderson poverty inquiry was initially established by conservative Liberal Prime Minister William McMahon in August 1972 before having its terms of reference expanded after Whitlam became Prime Minister in December of the same year (Regan & Stanton, 2019). Ultimately, the Inquiry was wide-ranging, involving substantial research and nation-wide consultation before producing a final report and sweeping recommendations in 1975, extending to policies regarding social security, employment services, housing affordability, marginalised populations, and more. Saunders (2019, p. 19) described Henderson's understanding of poverty, reflected in the Inquiry's reports, as something that:

> ...grates with the neoliberal agenda that has [since] come to dominate economic and social policy, which adopts a deficit approach to poverty that sees its causes as individual, reflecting a combination of poor choices, lack of planning and motivation and an unending appetite to live off the public purse. Bludgers.

Indeed, as the Henderson Inquiry (1975, p. 132) noted:

> ... It is unjust to blame people for being out of work when there are no jobs, when the available jobs are inaccessible, when the jobs are not suitable for unskilled and semi-skilled workers, or when the health of the workers concerned is not good enough for them to hold a regular job.

Subsequently, structural causes of poverty were given primary attention in the Inquiry, including the ways in which the social security system is imbued with patriarchal understandings of women's roles and needs that contribute to women's economic insecurity. By way of example, the Henderson Inquiry recommended that definitions guiding payment types should remove "those features of the social security system which seem to imply that man is the breadwinner and women necessarily his dependent chattel" (Henderson Inquiry, 1975, p. 53). The final report also recommended that:

> The independence of women can … be increased by raising the proportion of the determined entitlement actually paid to the wife [sic.] at the expense of the husband's [sic.] share.
>
> (Henderson Inquiry, 1975, p. 42)

The Henderson Inquiry was recently described by former Australian Deputy Prime Minister, Brian Howe (2024, p. 906) as "the most coherent, thoroughly researched basis for social policy Australia has seen". In the Inquiry's main report, which addressed income poverty, proposals included recommendations[9] that Australia adopt a GMI with a primary aim of providing adequate income support so that Australians would not fall into poverty (Henderson Inquiry, 1975; Ingles et al., 2019). The proposed GMI, which has been described as similar to a UBI (Henderson, 2019; Howe 2018a, 2018b; Ingles et al., 2019), was to involve an automatic payment of a minimum income to all (i.e., "non-categorical payments", for which no application would be required), including higher rates to some categories of people, such as pensioners and those with disability (i.e., "categorical payments", for which an application would be required) (Saunders, 1981). Non-categorical payments were to be set at between 62% and 71% of the Henderson poverty line,[10] depending on the number of children being cared for, while categorical GMI payments were to be set at 106% of the Henderson poverty line (Saunders, 1981). Moreover, with a linear tax rate of 40% on all private income (i.e., not including GMI income) and a surtax on high incomes, the GMI was designed to be "self-financing" (Ingles et al., 2019; Saunders, 1981, p. 23). In this respect, the GMI would have involved integration between the income tax and social security systems whereby income tax was proposed as the means of recouping GMI payments from those who had private sources of income (e.g., employment), and where the tax rate would be set in relation to financing needs for GMI payments (Saunders, 1981). Ultimately, for the GMI, "The minimum income payment levels are set to ensure all income units are raised above the poverty line, either automatically in the case of categorical units, or when supplemented at least by minimum wages for non-categorical units" (Saunders, 1981, p. 23). The latter was not true, however, for some individuals (e.g., those with six or more children) (Saunders, 1981).

The GMI scheme was proposed to be paid at the household unit level, with the typical unit defined as a nuclear family of a husband, wife, and dependent children, reflecting dominant social mores at the time (Saunders, 1981). This stands in contrast to UBI, which is defined by BIEN (2023) as an individual payment—a point that I return to in later chapters. The Commission did acknowledge, however, that payments might also be made directly to older children, while mothers might also be able to directly receive the "family allowance" proportion of the GMI (i.e., the proportion of the proposed payment that was introduced as a Family Allowances Scheme in 1976) (Saunders, 1981). As Saunders (1981, p. 25) noted, arguments against paying the GMI at the family unit level include the possibility that this might "impose additional inefficiencies in respect of the work incentives of married women and add considerably to the administrative complexity of the tax system".[11] Indeed, another primary goal of the GMI was to *reduce* administrative complexity, in order to make the tax and social security systems easier to understand, more accessible, more efficient, and less costly (Ingles et al., 2019; Saunders, 1981). As Saunders (1981, pp. 26–27) argued, "avoiding complicated investigative procedures required to establish eligibility, a simple system can [also] reduce, if not eliminate, the stigma associated with the current [social security] system".

Despite the promise of the GMI proposal to go some way towards addressing poverty in Australia, including for women and First Nations peoples, it was never implemented in practice. According to Howe (2013), the recommendations of the Henderson poverty inquiry were not given serious consideration by the conservative Fraser Government (1975–1983), which immediately followed the Whitlam Government's 1975 infamous sacking by the Australian Governor-General. Saunders (1998, p. 65) described the GMI proposal as being nearly immediately "dead in the water"; a "moderately radical reform" (Saunders, 1981, p. 27) that was never pursued. As described earlier, in the decades that have followed the Henderson poverty inquiry and its GMI proposal, Australian social security has endured significant changes which partly reflect changes in the Australian population, but also the growing influence of neoliberalism. Arguably, and as emerges from the stories told by women in subsequent chapters, these changes have served to reinforce the potential advantages of a UBI as a counterpoint for Australia.

Conclusion

The Australian social security system has undergone major reform since its gradual emergence after federation, particularly in the post-WWII period, during the Whitlam era, and again in recent decades. Across this time, impacts upon women have differed and, although significant advancements were made by the Whitlam Government, these have been largely (though certainly not entirely) eroded in the ensuing decades. For women, and particularly First Nations women, the punitiveness of Australian social security policies is now keenly and disproportionately felt, producing myriad harms, and often worsening, rather than alleviating, poverty and economic insecurity (Staines et al., 2024).

The Henderson Inquiry's proposal for a GMI represented a potential "fork in the road": something that differed dramatically from Australian social security policy developments of subsequent decades. Whether a UBI might offer a similar opportunity to improve conditions for Australian women into the future remains an open question. As set out in Chapter 1, the subsequent chapters of this book further explore this, drawing on the stories of the 26 women who participated in research interviews to discuss a hypothetical UBI for Australia. The next chapter first considers how, within the sociopolitical context described above, a UBI might affect Australian women's economic security.

Notes

1 For example, Maternity Payments (from 1912), the national Child Endowment Allowance (1941–1976), Wife's Allowance (from 1943), War Widow's Pension (from 1917), and Widow's Pension (from 1941).

2 As Jordens (1999, p. 26) sets out, "From 1844, the naturalisation laws of the Australian colonies were directed towards aliens and, with the exception of Western Australia, made no mention of Aborigines [*sic.*]. Prior to 1921, Indigenous Australians denied citizenship under colony or State law had to apply to be come naturalised British subjects in Australia in the same way as aliens. Under the *Nationality Act 1920* (Cth), all Aborigines [*sic.*] and Torres Strait Islanders born after January 1, 1921 gained the status of British subjects. In 1949, therefore, they automatically became Australian citizens under the *Nationality and Citizenship Act 1948* (Cth)". They did not, however, enjoy the citizenship rights that others were able to claim (Jordens, 1999; Moreton-Robinson 2009).

3 For example, in relation to Aboriginal and Torres Strait Islander peoples, this included: enacting anti-discrimination legislation; allocating funding for Aboriginal and Torres Strait Islander legal support; establishing a National Aboriginal Consultative Committee; returning the lands of the Gurindji peoples to traditional ownership; and drafting *The Aboriginal Land (Northern Territory) Bill*, which enabled land rights to be granted to Aboriginal and Torres Strait Islander peoples (Hocking, 2018). Guugu Yimithirr man, Noel Pearson, paid homage to this legacy in the eulogy he gave upon Whitlam's passing in 2014 as follows:

> Without this old man the land and human rights of our people would never have seen the light of day... The Whitlam government is the textbook case of reform trumping management. In less than three years an astonishing reform agenda leapt off the policy platform and into legislation and the machinery of programs of government. The country would change forever. The modern cosmopolitan Australia finally emerged like a technicolour butterfly from its long dormant chrysalis (Pearson, 2014).

4 This remains the case today: https://www.csmc.org.au/

5 For instance, the removal of tertiary education fees, increased expenditure on public housing, and ballooning of expenditure on early childhood services, which had dramatic impacts for women in particular (Brennan, 2019; Marston & Staines, 2020).

6 Though this waiting period was removed from the Supporting Parents Benefit in 1980 (McDonald & Spindler, 1988).

7 While prior to 1986/1987 a dependent student aged 16–25 years might also be considered a "child" for the purposes of the benefit, the child subsequently had to be aged 16 or less from this time on (McDonald & Spindler, 1988).

8 For a transcript of former Prime Minister Julia Gillard's historical "misogyny speech" in the Australian Parliament on 9 October 2012, see here: https://www.smh.com.au/politics/federal/transcript-of-julia-gillards-speech-20121010-27c36.html

9 The proposed GMI was canvassed in recommendations 1, 2, 6, 9, 10, 11, 12, and 13 (Henderson, 1975; Saunders, 1981).

10 The Henderson poverty line was developed as an output of the Henderson poverty inquiry. Despite critiques, it is still widely relied upon today. For an overview of the history of the Henderson poverty line, see: https://melbourneinstitute.unimelb.edu.au/research/labour/henderson-poverty-line. For updated reporting on poverty line rates, see here: https://melbourneinstitute.unimelb.edu.au/publications/poverty-lines

11 Although a tax credit of 20% of waged income for "working wives" was also proposed by the Henderson Inquiry, to alleviate this risk (Ingles et al., 2019).

3 Women's economic (in)security

> I think a lot of women are in similar circumstances to me where they've taken time out of the workforce or greatly reduced their hours. And so their long-term career progression, their long-term ability to earn a higher salary, super, all of that decreased.
>
> (Marley, 35 years)

International human rights instruments, including the *International Covenant on Economic, Social and Cultural Rights* (1966) and the *Convention on the Elimination of All Forms of Discrimination Against Women* (1979), contain provisions that protect economic rights. Article 3 of both treaties, for instance, obliges signatory states—including Australia—to safeguard equal access to economic rights for all, including (under the Convention) to take "all appropriate measures… to ensure the full development and advancement of women, for the purpose of guaranteeing them the exercise and enjoyment of human rights and fundamental freedoms on a basis of equality with men". Such rights underpin economic security, a broader concept encompassing both the ability to cover "essential needs sustainably and with dignity" (ICRC, 2015), and the affective experience of being able to do so (Rohde et al., 2015). Economic insecurity, by contrast, involves "the sense of stress or anxiety experienced by individuals when faced with inadequately insured economic risk", the latter of which stem from chronic conditions (e.g., low pay/income, high living/housing costs, limited savings), sudden shocks (e.g., job loss, relationship breakdown), or a mixture of both (Rohde et al., 2015).

Despite international standards and growing recognition of economic security's importance, sex remains a key predictor of economic outcomes. As discussed in earlier chapters, Australia—despite being a signatory to both abovementioned treaties[1]—has a national gender pay gap (considering total remuneration) of 21.8% ($28,425 per annum) (WGEA, 2024). For First Nations women, median weekly total personal income is 23.7% less than for non-Indigenous women and 47.8% less when compared with

DOI: 10.4324/9781003586593-3

all men (Australian Government, 2024). Moreover, women transitioning from partnerships to singlehood experience an average 16.7% reduction in household income compared with a mere 0.2% for men. For single *mothers*, this reduction in household income upon separating climbs to 20% (Australian Government, 2024). Although these gaps are narrowing, progress is painfully slow. So much so that the current child-bearing generation cannot reasonably expect their children or grandchildren to see full parity in their lifetimes. While governments across the world continue to emphasise women's economic security, they must also question whether the prevailing focus on increasing workforce participation is sufficient, given the sluggish pace of change.

It is within this context that this chapter explores the possible impacts of a UBI on Australian women's economic (in)security in both the short and long term. First, I discuss how a UBI might contribute to valuing unpaid care work that is disproportionately undertaken by women. Although most women interviewed for this book agreed this would be a particularly beneficial outcome of a UBI for Australia, there are also caveats to this approach. Second, I turn to the possible impacts of a UBI on Australian women's experiences with paid work, often in lower-paid feminised sectors. Reflecting broader UBI research, participants highlighted the potential for a UBI to provide a baseline of economic security, enabling them to make different employment choices. Third, and picking up on some of the content covered in Chapter 2, I canvass women's views about how a UBI might help circumvent what they overwhelmingly see as harmful, miserly, and stigmatising interactions with Australia's social security system. Before discussing these three core themes, however, I initially turn to whether and how the specific hypothetical UBI scenario used in this study ($1,203 per fortnight) might affect women's self-reported economic security, overall. The following section responds to this question, providing a foundation for exploring the detailed mechanisms through which a UBI might shape economic security in the remainder of the chapter.

An Australian UBI and women's overall economic security

Both income and wealth—the latter including accumulated cash and financial assets—combine to shape perceptions of economic security. However, income has the greatest influence (Kendall et al., 2018). Amongst the 26 women interviewed for this study, average income was $51,444 per annum, with a range of $0–$240,000 per annum (see Appendix 1). This is slightly lower than the average taxable income of all Australian women ($60,054 per annum), which is lower again than for all Australian men ($84,326 per annum) (Australian Tax Office, 2024). Given this, most of the women interviewed here might report a lower baseline level of economic security than would otherwise be found in the general population. However, our primary focus was on how the proposed UBI might shape women's subjective sense of economic security, regardless of their baseline income. To examine this, we asked women, at the beginning of each interview, to indicate their current economic security, and to consider how it might change with the hypothetical fortnightly UBI payment.

To ensure consistency across women's responses, we asked them to indicate their level of economic security against a purpose-built economic security rating scale, ranging from 1 (economically *in*secure) to 10 (economically secure) (see Appendix 1 for an image of this scale). At the "economically *insecure*" end of the scale, the following examples were included to anchor women's understanding of what it might mean to be economically insecure:

- "difficult to make ends meet",
- "vulnerable to economic shocks (e.g., big bills, loss of income)", and
- "have few sources of support in times of economic need".

In contrast, at the "economically secure" end of the scale, the opposite statements were displayed ("easy to make ends meet", "resilient to economic shocks [e.g., big bills, loss of income]", "have many sources of support in times of economic need"). The statements accorded with how economic security has been measured elsewhere (e.g., Rohde et al., 2015). We reminded women to rate themselves individually, rather than considering overall household incomes (where these were present), so that we could isolate women's discrete situations.

Most women had no trouble articulating where they thought they sat on the scale. However, for others this was more difficult, and their rating was nevertheless influenced by whether they lived with others who had higher incomes, since this meant they could also answer "yes" to "having many sources of support in times of economic need". For instance, Terri (30 years) explained:

Terri:	I think it's hard for me to answer this as an individual... [because] although I earn 40k [per annum], yeah, my household income is around 180k [per annum] for my partner's income. So, I would rate an eight or a nine on this scale because of that...
Interviewer:	I appreciate that response. I wonder if, though, I might be able to get you to rate yourself just as an individual...
Terri:	I think including supports outside of the household, I'd probably say I'm a seven.

As this interaction demonstrates, rating scales of this nature are never an exact science. However, this exercise nevertheless gives us a high-level indication of change.

In relation to their current state of economic security (i.e., *without* the hypothetical UBI), women reported an average response of 4.46/10. With a rating of 1 indicating very poor economic security, and a rating of 10 indicating strong economic security, women's average of 4.46 showed that they did experience relative economic insecurity, overall. Indeed, as outlined above, many of the women reported relatively low incomes (particularly those receiving social security) and said that they experience significant stress around the (in)stability of these. For instance, nearly all women, even those with higher incomes, spoke about their concerns around sudden and unexpected changes to their health, family situation or more, which could derail their economic security—particularly changes that might leave them unable (or less able) to perform wage work and/or that might increase their share of unpaid care work. For Jules (30 years), who suffers from several health issues, "it's not a sure thing that I'll be able to work next month or in a year or 10 years from now", which creates an "underlying kind of fear" and stress. For others with poor health who receive disability support pension (DSP) social security payments, such as Pat (52 years), the fear of losing their income—either via policy reform, or reassessments of individual eligibility by social security service delivery agency, Centrelink—also causes significant ongoing worry about the ability to maintain economic security. As DSP recipient Eva (58 years) put it, "It really isn't hard to see, losing everything". This is particularly acute, given frequent changes and ever-increasing restrictions on access to Australia's DSP over the past decade or more, as I expand on later (Collie et al., 2021).

Although issues with DSP are discrete, in many ways, women's overall views reflect a more generalised intensification of precariousness resulting from significant economic and social transformations that have impacted Australians in recent decades. This includes the more general erosion in Australia (and other similar welfare states) of social security safety nets (described in Chapter 2), but also the significant deregulation of the Australian labour market from the late 1980s onwards alongside the associated rise of so-called "precarious" employment (Bessant & Watts, 2021; Briggs & Buchanan, 2000; Parfitt & Barnes, 2020; Standing, 2011). For women, the impacts of these changes are even more palpable, because economic reserves are generally weaker in the first place. For First Nations women, who tend to have even fewer reserves still, this is often even more profound.

The UBI amount proposed here (i.e., \$1,203 per fortnight/\$31,278 per annum) would represent a substantial increase to the incomes of most women in this study. Based on the participants' average per annum income, the hypothetical UBI would amount to an average increase of ~61% (or 13% for even the highest paid individual). This was reflected in women's changed responses regarding their economic security, when taking this hypothetical UBI into account. Overall, their self-reported economic security increased with the UBI by 2.29 points on average, from 4.46/10 to 6.75/10 (min=3, max=10): a substantial improvement of just over 51%. Overwhelmingly, the idea of this improved economic security prompted palpable emotional reactions; women said that they would feel sheer relief, and major reductions in stress, worry, and anxiety (something I return to in Chapter 5). Bindi (31 years) explained, "That would make me feel so much relief... it would allow me to just be myself and not try and have mental backflips all the time... I wouldn't be so worried for my future". Similarly, for Holly (27 years) the UBI would "remove a lot of stress". This was often the case for women whose economic security was mediated by their ability to juggle unpaid care alongside employment, as I turn to below.

UBI and caregiving

In nearly all interviews for this study, and reflecting existing research, women positioned UBI as an important means of remunerating unpaid work, including volunteering, but especially caregiving. As per the quote from Marley (35 years) that appeared at the beginning of this chapter, there was widespread recognition that it remains predominantly women who take time away from paid work to absorb the responsibilities of caregiving—whether for children, loved ones, or others—which thereby affects their earnings, career progression, and savings. Indeed, worldwide in 2020, women spent about three times more hours than men on unpaid domestic work and care: approximately 4.2 versus 1.7 hours per day (United Nations, 2020). The situation is similar in Australia, where women also provide far higher levels of unpaid care than Australian men, with Aboriginal and Torres Strait Islander women undertaking the highest amounts of unpaid care in the country (Hunter et al., 2016; Klein et al., 2024; Yap & Biddle, 2012). As shown in a recent study I undertook with colleagues (Klein et al., 2024), unpaid caregiving accounts for anywhere between 40% and 62% of Indigenous women's time on an average weekday. When compared with national data, this is roughly double that of non-Indigenous women (Klein et al., 2024).

Women spoke about how a UBI might assist with caregiving in two ways, each of which I tackle separately in the remainder of this sub-section. First, it may provide some level of remuneration for work that is currently unpaid, thereby enabling caregivers to partially recoup forgone incomes, while also "celebrating" the importance of care work in a way that is not currently the case under normative institutional settings. Second, it may ease women's ability to purchase commodified care (e.g., childcare, aged care), which would reduce their own responsibility for providing this care in an unpaid capacity.

UBI and unpaid care

UBI was regularly positioned as "celebrat[ing] the non-paid jobs that people do" (Emma, 33 years), by way of providing at least some level of remuneration. For instance, as Alex (63 years) explained, a UBI would give people the freedom and time to be able to provide care without facing possible destitution. Kiah (39 years) invoked the "sandwich generation" concept (Alburez-Gutierrez et al., 2021), talking about how women often simultaneously care for elderly adults *as well as* children, leaving little time for other things, including paid work. As she sees it, "I don't think in a lot of Australian communities we know how to do aging well" (Kiah). Indeed, appropriate care infrastructures are not necessarily available to support people to "age in place" and moreover, the standards of commodified aged care facilities have been shown to be alarmingly poor in recent inquiries (O'Loughlin et al., 2017; Royal Commission into Aged Care Quality and Safety, 2021). Across Australia, "sandwich generation" caregiving is becoming more common since "people are having children later, children are staying at home longer, and older Australians are living longer" (Kelsey-Sugg & Hunt, 2024). As O'Shea (cited in Kelsey-Sugg & Hunt, 2024) explained, "Women make up 91 per cent of 'sandwich' carers, and 40 per cent of those women also have paid jobs", with significant negative health impacts of having to balance what are often incredibly high care loads against paid work. Although not currently part of the sandwich generation, Marley (35 years), who has multiple children, including one with disability, changed her employment to part-time to accommodate care for her children. Meanwhile, her partner continues to work full-time:

> I definitely do 90% of the mental load and admin part of it [caregiving for the children]. And the physical part of it is probably a more even split, probably. I don't know. Maybe 60/40, with me 60. Oh, I think I'm being too generous there really, but yes... So yeah, I do [the] majority and I'm the one who generally has to work around all of that other stuff and juggle and move things and yeah... He [partner] does, on occasion, take carer's leave, sick leave, or sometimes works from home, but nowhere near the amount that I do. And it's always me who has to initiate that rather than it just being done.

Because one of her children lives with disability, the administrative load associated with Marley's caregiving role is sometimes huge:

> When you have a child with disability, regardless of what that disability is, you're more likely to have increased medical appointments and often specialists, increased costs… So, it's managing all of those appointments. Generally there's a lot more communication and support required from schools and daycares. So it's also a matter of liaising, being the one [to] liaise between all these different professionals, keeping them all in the loop, booking appointments, and everyone has waiting lists. So it's going on waiting lists, managing appointments, taking what you can get, which is often in work hours… And that's just normal. When there's also things that are more challenging or a crisis, it's increasing all of that…

Marley's child receives support through Australia's National Disability Insurance Scheme (NDIS), which I discuss further in Chapter 5. Aligning with other research into the NDIS, however, this adds to Marley's care-related administrative burden because it requires her to manage NDIS claims, provide documentation, keep track of her child's NDIS budget and more (Carey et al., 2021; Dickinson & Yates, 2023; DPM&C, 2023). Marley also receives a government-provided Carer Allowance of $159.30 each fortnight, which she describes as "a minimal amount", but which does help. In contrast, the larger UBI amount would provide far greater support and, to some extent, replace the income Marley has lost by moving to part-time employment to accommodate her caregiving. Many other women described similar scenarios. For Terri (30 years), the hypothetical UBI would support her and her partner to more effectively act as kinship carers for two children who live with them intermittently. For single parent, Alex (63 years), a UBI would have meant being able to build up more savings to improve economic security for her and her child, including later in life. In this sense, a UBI was positioned as being able to not only better support women who provide care, but to also "save society money" by improving the health and well-being of those both giving and receiving care (Alex, 63 years). Nevertheless, whether a UBI, such as that proposed here, represents a sufficient level of remuneration for those undertaking unpaid care is questionable.

Across Australia, the total market value of unpaid care work has been estimated at $650.1 billion per annum, which is equivalent to ~50.6% of Australia's Gross Domestic Product (WGEA, 2016). In the study into Aboriginal and Torres Strait Islander women's care that I referred to above (Klein et al., 2024), we estimated that the market value of unpaid care work was somewhere between $223.01 and $457.39 per day, representing an annual estimated salary of between \$81,175.64 and \$118,921.40 per person. For Indigenous women alone, this represents somewhere between ~\$33 and \$48 billion per annum across Australia. It is harder, of course, to also estimate the incredible social and cultural value of this labour. Nevertheless, these approximations give some indication of the astonishing contribution that unpaid care makes to the economy writ large, and thus—as Fraser (2016) describes it—the extent to which the economy "free rides" on this unpaid work. Put into context, then, in terms of providing some level of direct remuneration for unpaid care, the UBI proposed here (\$1,203 per fortnight/\$31,278 per annum) is relatively small, representing for example somewhere between 26% and 39% of the estimated foregone salaries outlined above. Those receiving a UBI in lieu of paid work will also forego other benefits of wage labour, including paid leave, wage growth, superannuation, and more (Miller et al., 2023; Roebyns, 2000; Widerquist, 2018; Zelleke, 2008, 2018).

This concern is borne out in recent study findings, which show that both "care incomes" (that is, incomes paid only to those who provide otherwise unpaid care) and UBI would improve women's overall income and thereby strengthen their economic security in the short term, but that by directing women out of the labour force, they would have longer-term negative impacts (Bibler et al., 2023; Cieplinski et al., 2023; Gibson et al., 2020). As Gibson et al. (2020) found, especially women with younger children will tend to respond to UBI by reducing their hours of paid employment, choosing instead to spend more time providing unpaid care. Similarly, de Paz-Báñez et al. (2020) reported slight decreases in labour supply for specific groups—including women with young children to care for (de Paz-Báñez et al., 2020). They also found, however, that these decreases are offset by increased labour supply across other groups, meaning UBI is unlikely to reduce labour force participation overall (de Paz-Báñez et al., 2020). While about half of the women interviewed here said they would reduce their paid work to make way for their caregiving, others had different views. For Tam (55 years), a UBI would provide a baseline level of security to be able to be "more entrepreneurial" in "expanding [their] business practice" and thus increasing their paid work. Nevertheless, for those who would reduce their paid work in response to UBI, there may be long-term negative consequences.

This reinforces warnings by some UBI scholars that the policy has the potential to further entrench rather than alleviate gendered norms around the distribution of paid and unpaid work, whereby women are freed up to do even *more* domestic and unpaid caregiving while men's roles remain largely unchanged (e.g., Miller et al., 2023; Roebyns, 2000; Zelleke, 2011). This possible outcome highlights that political and social constructions of motherhood continue to represent one of the most profound, deeply rooted, and relatively unquestioned indicators of sexism and enduring patriarchal structures across most societies (O'Reilly, 2010). Indeed, women in this study tended to internalise rather than disrupt hegemonic social constructions of motherhood/womanhood. Eva (58 years), for example, repeatedly referred to women as "the nurturers of … children", and where others *did* comment on the unfairness of unequal gendered distributions of unpaid labour, they nevertheless still appeared to internalise/perpetuate normative gender roles when arguing for or against the importance of UBI in this regard. For example:

> I've got to do all this housework and look after the kids because [my] husband thinks he's something special and doesn't have to do it. I can't go back to work as well. [So I'd think] "Thank God there's a universal basic income that I get each week".
>
> (Erica, 65 years)

> Men don't have to do that [care for children and parents]. Right? They just get looked after all their life. So I think women would really benefit more with this than men would.
>
> (Alex, 63 years)

Meanwhile, the notion that caregiving might be prioritised by all genders *alongside* paid work (as per Fraser's [1997] "universal caregiver" model) was not explicitly raised in relation to care during the interviews.

Care work is crucial to the functioning of our societies, involving the material and affective labour that "forms capitalism's human subjects" (Fraser, 2016, n.p.). And yet, as discussed earlier, capitalist economies extract much of this labour for free, dismissing it as inessential and/or unproductive (Federici, 1975; Fraser, 2016, n.p.). This is a deeply entrenched social norm, which is difficult to shift. Indeed, often while seeking improved economic security for women, much feminist scholarship continues to perpetuate the devaluing of care as a "burden" that should (at least in part) be reduced and redistributed (e.g., Elson, 2017). A 2018 United Nations Development Programme report on women's care, for instance, provides a good example, with its title reading: *Now is the time! Reduce and redistribute the unpaid domestic and care work burden of women for sustainable development.* However, this approach fails to reflect caregiving as strength and as something that "defines human value" (Klein et al., 2024; Kleinman, 2012, p. 1550). It also fails to incorporate different views about the value and importance of care in society.

As Miller et al. (2023, p. 187) note in relation to the 1960s–1970s welfare claimants' movement in the United States, although white middle-class feminists were fighting to reduce their caregiving roles to make way for entry into the labour market, "Black welfare recipients wanted the option to care for their own children, rather than working outside the home [often caring for others' children or houses], a privilege that white middle-class women had long enjoyed". Similarly, in our recent study referred to earlier (Klein et al., 2024), women regularly spoke about care as being central and core to societal well-being. From this perspective, all genders need greater support in their care, rather than being viewed primarily as breadwinners who simply provide care "on the side". This again echoes Fraser's universal caregiver model, which elevates the value and importance of care, as well as the benefit of involving all genders in caregiving responsibilities (Fraser, 1997).

Ultimately, the benefit of a UBI is that it is flexible: it gives all individuals greater choice to decide for themselves whether and how to balance paid work with unpaid care. Nevertheless, it does little to tackle the norm that it is women who are primarily carers. It also fails to strike at the core of the problem itself, which is that caregiving is so grossly undervalued in our wage labour arrangements to begin with (Weeks, 2011). What our interviews with women do show is that in Australia, much work is still needed to continue to destabilise these entrenched social norms. Indeed, and as others have rightly claimed (Zelleke, 2011), a UBI alone cannot achieve true gender equality. Even though the potential of UBI to redistribute unpaid labour was not at the forefront of interviewees' minds, what *did* repeatedly arise was the potential of UBI to support the purchasing of commodified forms of care, which may have other tangible impacts for women.

UBI and commodified care

The term "commodified care" refers to forms of care that are purchased on the market, including childcare, aged care, and more. As opposed to the unpaid care discussed earlier, commodified care is typically waged. In Australia, increasing access to commodified forms of care has been a primary strategy for moving more women into the labour force and, in turn, closing the gender pay gap. As Australian Treasurer Jim Chalmers put it in a 2022 speech to an International Women's Day leadership forum:

> In the Global Gender Gap report for 2021, Australia recorded its worst ever result—falling to 50th place... How are we going to address this? ... First, by dismantling barriers to participation... This is not just about primary carers joining the labour market. It's about

> fuller participation in terms of more hours and in the jobs they [women] aspire to... We won't be able to make the labour pool bigger while childcare costs—the single biggest barrier to work facing single parents and primary carers—are skyrocketing at almost double CPI [consumer price index], like they have been over the past year.

Chalmers was touching on issues, however, that have been front and centre in Australian politics for some decades now (Brennan, 1998), including again in the lead up to a 2025 Australian federal election (Gould, 2025). The cost and availability of childcare were also raised by several women interviewees. As Hannah (42 years) and others (e.g., Alex, 63 years) noted, high costs are a significant barrier to accessing childcare and often delay primary caregivers' decisions to return to paid work. As Alex recounted, the costs of childcare have increased exponentially since her child was young, making it much "harder for women now" than it used to be. The Australian Government provides a means-tested Childcare Subsidy to those who are eligible, though even with the subsidy, out-of-pocket costs can still be prohibitive. Kiah (39 years) explained:

> I still have a child in childcare. And even with the Childcare Subsidy that we get, it is offensively expensive. But at the same time, if you don't have family to lean on, and you work full time, that's just kind of what you've got to do. So, at the end of the day or the end of the fortnight or month, [the] reality is how much [financial] inroads are you actually making?

Recently, political editor for the Australian Financial Review, Coorey (2024), described the Australian childcare sector as "...a mess of largely privately operated centres, which pay their workers peanuts and charge parents a fortune, mainly to cover the costs of real estate and compliance". Considering that Australia's national average cost for long day care is around $135 per day, total childcare costs without any Childcare Subsidy for a full-time placement can be up to $35,100 per annum (Care for Kids, 2025). The hypothetical UBI considered here would cover 89% of these annual costs, which roughly accords with the amount those claiming the full subsidy rate of 90% per annum currently receive (i.e., those with family annual incomes between $0 and $83,280) (Services Australia, 2024b). A UBI would, however, be provided without means testing (unlike the Childcare Subsidy) (Australian Government, 2025). Furthermore, a UBI provided *in addition to* existing schemes would undoubtedly improve childcare affordability. Nevertheless, cost is not the only barrier to childcare access. Indeed, being able to secure a spot in a childcare facility is also an increasing problem for Australian parents, with so-called childcare "deserts" becoming more frequent across Australia (Fuller, 2024). This often means that even if parents sign their children up for childcare before they are even born, they may still not have secured a childcare place for them by the time they are ready to return to work (Finlay in Fuller, 2024). While a UBI may assist with the cost barrier to access, other reforms are needed to improve availability. Similarly, ongoing reforms are needed to ensure Australian childcare centres are safe, healthy, and nurturing places for children—especially given recent reports of abuse (Australian Human Rights Commission 2025).

Reforms to Australia's early childhood care system are ongoing, including in response to a recent Productivity Commission (2024) inquiry, recommending pathways towards a universal system. However, whether Australia heads in this direction is yet to be seen. The inquiry also made recommendations about improving early childhood sector working conditions and pay—something that would disproportionately affect women, who represent most staff across the sector. This taps into another key theme that appeared in women's conversations about UBI: its potential to improve women's experiences of paid work.

Improving paid work

Prabhakar (2020) argues that for women, who tend to be overrepresented as employees in lower-paying sectors and in precarious work, UBI offers a relatively stable supplement to improve economic security (also Campbell & Burgess, 2018; Chung, 2023; Cuesta & Pico, 2020; Foley & Cooper, 2021; Schulz, 2017; Sharma & Rawal, 2022). In addition to being low-paid, Prabhakar (2020) notes that feminised sectors are also disproportionately affected by global crises (e.g., COVID-19), meaning the additional economic protection of a UBI is even more desperately needed (also see Wood et al., 2021). This was also raised by around a third of the women interviewed here. As Kiah (39 years) put it, for example:

> ...the gender difference of Australia's industries... Thinking about childcare workers, I think there's questions around [whether] they're one of the lowest paid sectors in the country and yet that's such a pivotal sector. So... if we follow that thought through, how something like this [UBI] ultimately would have a greater benefit to ... women working in the industries that are skewed towards women...

In the most recent available data from 2018, a significant proportion of Australia's workforce outside of the public sector was segmented by sex, with women disproportionately represented in lower-paid care and education sectors (see Appendix 4). Even within female-dominated industries, women are lower paid than men (see Appendix 5). This is, in part, related to a persistent "glass ceiling" effect, whereby women are underrepresented in managerial and leadership roles. For instance, in 2018, women made up a mere 17.1% of Chief Executive Officers (CEOs) across all industries (excluding the public sector), and only 30.5% of overall "key management personnel" (e.g., those who "have authority and responsibility for planning, directing and controlling the activities of the entity, directly or indirectly…") (WGEA, 2019, n.p.). This arises from a mix of factors, including higher responsibility for unpaid caregiving, higher rates of part-time and casual work (often to accommodate caregiving roles), workplace discrimination and more (Evans & Maley, 2020; WGEA, 2019). In relation to workplace discrimination, Evans and Maley (2020, p. 213) explain that "unconscious bias against women … result[s] from persistent stereotypes about gender roles and the desired qualities of leaders that remain entrenched despite the significant gains that have been made in women's educational achievement and participation in non-traditional careers". As with social norms around caregiving, a UBI alone cannot hope to address gender-based discrimination. Nevertheless, it may empower workers to make different choices about their paid work.

Women's stories of navigating paid work were rife with examples of discrimination on multiple levels—not just related to gender, but also related to age, disability, caregiver status, and more. For Fiona (60 years), age discrimination had punctuated her experience of looking for work. She explained:

> …then at the age of 60, even getting your CV looked at is not that easy anymore. I've cut off 20 years off my CV so that there's no assumptions made about my age and things like that but that is serious… For a professional person, which I consider myself, my ability to get work that fits my skills and experience is really curtailed by my age…
>
> (Fiona, 60 years)

Fiona, who is a cancer survivor, is in the situation of having to look for work because she was laid off by her previous employer:

> I used to make this joke when they were laying off people all the time and while I was off sick and say, "Oh, they're not going to sack the chick with cancer", and then they did.

For Hannah (42 years), a UBI might have helped her escape an employer who discriminated against her due to her disability, and against whom she "lodged a disability discrimination complaint". Touching on issues around violence against women, which I expand on in Chapter 4, Gabbi (38 years) explained how she thought a UBI might also help women escape unsafe workplaces:

> I think it also, in terms of the workplace, would mean we're not as worried when we get sexually harassed or bullied because [we could quit] ... I think it would do a lot to stop the abuse that's inherent in the society that we're in.

Casey (47 years), who is a mother of a transgender child, told the story of a previous workplace, where she experienced persistent and ongoing discrimination and violence:

> I worked through the same-sex marriage plebiscite [held in late 2017] in a small building within a team of extremely transphobic, racist, sexist, everything co-workers. It was an extremely difficult time for me as the mother of a trans child, and as a bisexual person, but mostly as the mother of a trans child. My direct coordinator told me that children would transition [their gender] over her dead body. People that I worked with who had absolutely no stake in whether or not LGBTQIA+ people exist or not had such violent opinions and took violent action at the time...
>
> At the time, I just sucked it up, and it took an enormous mental toll. I remember sometimes I used to ring helplines before I went to work, to psych myself up to be able to go to work. Ultimately, I made a complaint, and a couple of other employees within the team made complaints also. And those complaints were never addressed properly at all... later on, I was threatened by a senior manager for speaking out. I would've left if I could have. But I couldn't, because you can't just quit a job... if I had left my job at that time, I would've started studying at that time, and I wouldn't have gone on to be harmed in my workplace for years after that...

Casey went on to emphasise:

> ... if I had had access to a universal basic income those years ago, roughly about five years ago now, I wouldn't have been harmed in my workplace for the last five years. I wouldn't been in the position that I'm in now. I would've started and completed my university study, and I would've had the option of going and working in a totally different industry in a safer workplace. And I could have worked forever.

In Casey's (47 years) view, the current system "fails people, because it really gives employers a lot of power". In a more general sense,

Casey (47 years) explained that a UBI might provide greater leverage to "marginalised communities who are often harmed and discriminated against in workplaces, because it would mean they would have choice about employment... they would be able to leave harmful employers". She went on:

> Because it means that workers would have some form of power. Workers would have some kind of financial security behind them when they face discrimination in the workplace... I think it [UBI] would compel employers to treat workers better...
>
> (Casey, 47 years)

This aligns with broader research on UBI, which indicates that it offers people—and particularly minority, poor, and migrant women—greater leverage in their choice of employment (Bibler et al., 2022; Vollenweider, 2017). Indeed, "reducing uncertainty and precariousness allow a longer-term outlook", which can have "significant impacts on the nature of work and activity people pursue, with selection of more meaningful activities, such as caring and entrepreneurship, improving people's wellbeing further" (Johnson et al., 2021, p. 413). This presents a potential opportunity for women to choose work that not only provides subsistence, but that aligns with their values and avoids harm (Altman & Markham, 2019; Chung, 2023; Howard, 2015; Staines et al., 2021a; Vidojević & Chipkin, 2021; Warren, 2010; Weeks, 2020; Wolf & Willis, 2018;). Indeed, as Srnicek and Williams (2015, p. 88) put it, "UBI... unbinds the coercive aspects of wage labour" by providing a buffer of economic security.

This relates to the issue of workplace bargaining more generally, which has undergone significant change in Australia over recent decades. As Pocock et al. (2008) note, women in low-paid work have been disproportionately affected by Australia's flagging industrial relations policies, which have tended to further weaken Australian unions and prioritise the negotiation of individual workplace agreements between employers and employees, ignoring power imbalances in such negotiations. However, research shows that attention to employer/employee power relations is important. For instance, as Recalde and Vesterlund (2023: 470) note, "Men more than women succeed when negotiating over labor-market outcomes, and gender differences in negotiation likely contribute to the gender wage gap and to horizontal and vertical segregation in the labor market". A 2013–2014 national survey undertaken by Australia's Fair Work Commission, with 2,050 employers and 7,800 employees, bears this out (WGEA, 2018). Overall, it found that 42.6% of surveyed employees had individually negotiated their pay rate, with the remaining respondents having had their pay fixed to award rates and/or negotiated via collective bargaining arrangements (WGEA, 2018). Of those individually negotiating their pay rate, 35.8% were women and 51.3% were men. In total, 15.5% were successful in attaining a pay rise because of their individual negotiations, including 19.2% of men but only 12.7% of women (WGEA, 2018). This led the WGEA (2018, p. 2) to conclude that "negotiation is a contributing factor when it comes to the gender pay gap".

As Recalde and Vesterland (2023) argue, policy responses that take a "fix the women" approach, encouraging women to behave more like men during negotiations, tend to have limited success. Alternatively, greater attention must also be given to addressing structural contributors to these unequal outcomes. As suggested above, UBI might play a role in providing individuals with at least a small amount of stable income that might bolster their power, though other measures—such as supporting collective rather than individual bargaining agreements—are also needed as part of a broader mix of policies to support women's economic security into the future (Lazar, 2020; Recalde & Vesterland, 2023). Similarly important is ensuring social security programs that provide sufficient support for those who need to reduce and/or leave paid work, and which do so in ways that avoid harm and stigma. I touched on some of this in Chapter 2, but return to it below, this time exploring women's views about their own experiences with social security and the possible opportunities presented by UBI.

Supplementing shrinking and harmful social security nets

Under international human rights instruments, social security is understood as a fundamental right and means of protecting economic security and freedom through redistribution that alleviates poverty. Nevertheless, under neoliberal welfare reforms in states like Australia, the United Kingdom, and the United States, social security has been (re)framed as a form of residual state support rather than a core human right (Esping-Andersen, 1990). Moreover, and as discussed in greater detail in Chapter 2, under "neoliberal paternalism" (Soss et al., 2011), the state has not simply retreated but also strengthened its paternalism in efforts to pursue and enforce free-market capitalism. Indeed, across most (neo)liberal welfare states (Esping-Andersen, 1991; Cavadino & Dignan, 2006), including Australia, conditions attached to social security receipt have intensified in ways that require recipients to submit to the norms of capitalism. This might be through engaging in paid work and/or participating in mandatory employment preparation and training regimes to maintain eligibility for social security payments (Wacquant, 2009).

Internationally, such welfare reforms have been accompanied and enabled by discourses that represent those receiving social security as parasitically "dependent" upon the state (Cassiman, 2008; O'Connor, 2001). At worst, social security recipients are stigmatised as lazy, substance-addicted, and morally corrupt: "deadbeat dads", "welfare queens"[2] (Cassiman, 2008), "dole bludgers" (Archer, 2009), and "welfare cheats" (Devereux & Power, 2019). Frequently, these discourses disproportionately demonise women, with a particular emphasis on (single) mothers who are black and/or First Nations (Cammett, 2014; Cassiman, 2008; Moreton-Robinson, 2009; Sabbioni, 1996; Sheared, 1998). In an analysis of Australian Government press releases and media concerning welfare fraud from 1997 to 2014, for instance, Wilcock (2014, p. 190) concluded that:

> ...unlike their male counterparts, female [welfare] "cheats" are additionally subject to high-pitched moral condemnations about their presumed sexual deviance, selfishness, or maternal failings. This female "welfare cheat" fuses the neoliberal mantra of "personal responsibility", in which the "cheat" is unambiguously culpable, with gendered assumptions about "bad women"...

In addition to misrecognition and stigma arising from these discourses (Fraser, 1997), the economic impacts of welfare reforms have also had devastating effects (Blaxland, 2010; Walters, 2002). Women in this study frequently spoke about the potential that a UBI holds in relation to reducing the harms of engaging with Australia's social security system. This typically related to two sub-themes. First, a UBI such as that proposed in the scenario here (i.e., set at the poverty line) would, most of the time, represent a significant increase to those receiving Australian social security benefits. Second, the universality of a UBI would reduce the stigma associated with social security receipt because it would recast everyone as beneficiaries of government assistance (Korpi & Palme, 1998). In both instances, it is assumed that social security benefits roughly similar to what are currently available would remain as targeted payments for those in greater need (Stephens, 2019). This would mimic the structure of the Guaranteed Minimum Income (GMI) proposed by Australia's Henderson Poverty Inquiry in 1975, described in Chapter 2. That is, it would enable universal access to a secure and stable safety net, while still recognising differences in the form of continued categorical payments. Interviewees frequently noted the importance of this model, as opposed to one that replaces social security payments altogether.

Increasing material support

As outlined in Chapter 2, most Australian social security payments sit below the poverty line. For instance, in December 2024, the base payment rate (single) for JobSeeker unemployment benefit ($389 per week) was a mere 64% of the poverty line ($612.18 per week) (Melbourne Institute, 2023b). Many have argued that this is woefully inadequate (e.g., ACOSS, 2024a), and in May 2024, over 200 female leaders from across Australia co-signed a letter to Prime Minister Anthony Albanese calling for an increase in the rate of JobSeeker unemployment benefit payment and Youth Allowance payment to improve women's economic security; especially those escaping violence (see ACOSS, 2024b). In this letter, Australia's Sex Discrimination Commissioner Anna Cody stated:

> Raising JobSeeker and related payments to liveable levels in the federal budget would help lift about half a million women out of poverty. Bolstering women's economic security is crucial to giving them the means to leave and remain free of violence.
>
> (ACOSS, 2024b)

Even if the UBI considered here were received *without* additional social security, it would immediately lift all Australians to the poverty line. When received in addition to existing social security payments for those in greater need, it would ensure all were lifted *above* the poverty line—that is, to somewhere between 117% and 183% of the poverty line, depending on payment types and categories. This includes:

- 832,095 Australians (46% of whom are women) who subsist on base rate "JobSeeker" unemployment benefits ($389.00 per week), which currently sit at ~64% of the Henderson Poverty Line,
- 316,915 Australians (71% of whom are women) who rely on base rate Carer Payment ($523.55 per week), which currently sits at ~86% of the Henderson Poverty Line, and
- 323,755 Australians (94% of whom are women) who receive base rate Parenting Payment Single ($503.75 per week), which currently sits at ~82% of the Henderson Poverty Line (DSS, 2024; Melbourne Institute, 2023a).

As reported during previous temporary increases to Australian social security payments, such as those experienced during the COVID-19 pandemic where a range of social security benefits were essentially doubled, the social impacts are vast. These include reduced crime, improved access to healthy foods, reduced housing stress, improved mental and physical health, and more (Botha et al., 2022; Klein et al., 2022a, 2022b; Lewis

& Lee 2020; Phillips et al., 2020; Raynor & Panza 2021; Staines & Zahnow, 2022). The changes also resulted in a 17-year low poverty rate after nearly 20 years of little movement at all (ACOSS, 2022). This had significant impacts for women, as those who were more likely to have been on social security incomes to begin with due to poorer baseline economic security.

Returning, however, to the earlier statement by the Australian Sex Discrimination Commissioner, the rate of social security unemployment benefits is not the only issue resulting in an increased likelihood that Australian women will experience violence. Indeed, as I elaborate on in Chapter 4, and in addition to broader gender norms that support violence against women, rules built into the social security system also increase women's vulnerability. The conditionalities attached to social security payments can also be experienced as a source of violence in and of themselves, with women being more likely to bear the brunt. For example, in relation to Australia's "compulsory income management" program, which sees social security payments directed to cashless bank cards, colleagues and I previously found that women tend to talk about feeling like they had entered a "domestic violence relationship with the state itself" as a result of the policy (Staines et al., 2024, p. 13). Indeed, as one woman described it:

> ...at the [compulsory income management provider] office... They had this [sign] hanging up on the wall behind the lady. It was all about domestic abuse, like freedom is everything and "say no". I was like, "that's kind of hypocritical isn't it"? Because if my partner was doing this to me [controlling my money, like the state under compulsory income management], you'd be telling me to leave him. But because it's the government doing it, they're completely fine.
>
> (Staines et al., 2024, pp. 13–14)

Returning to this current study, Emma (33 years) put it bluntly, stating "I think the key lesson we can learn from the basic income and contrasting it to conditional payment is get rid of conditionality". Holly (27 years), a current social security recipient, explained:

> It would be a pretty big weight off my back. The mutual obligations are anxiety inducing because if something screws up anywhere in the system... and the system is not designed well. Those IT systems are running on... They're held together by gum and a couple of crushed hopes and dreams... Any failure in the IT system there means that my payment would be cut. It's happened before.
>
> (Holly, 27 years)

A previous suspension to her Centrelink payment, which was no fault of her own, meant that Holly was "hit with a heap of late fees and stuff like that" because her direct debits that she had set up to pay recurring bills "bounced" (Holly, 27 years). This is a common experience for Australian social security recipients, as reported elsewhere (e.g., Marston et al., 2022; Staines et al., 2024). Engaging with employment services also takes up huge amounts of time, making it difficult for social security recipients to do other crucial work, like care for children and/or plan towards building their own business. Tracy (46 years) spoke about having, in the past, received Parenting Payment *without* mutual obligations,[3] which felt similar to a UBI and enabled her to "build the first Mums in Business Network in Australia, and ... [win] business awards". As Tracy explained, at the time she:

> ...had that money to pay the bills while I was able to build that business. And that's one of the reasons I think basic income would be amazing because at the moment, I'm trying to get onto this self-employment thing [via Centrelink to ensure self-employment is a recognised mutual obligation activity], which is a nightmare to get on, but it's like, I know what I want to do, I just need those mutual obligations off my back for a while so I can build it [the business] up... I was [in the past] a parent to my children, but also I built this business... Then Julia Gillard [told me] to go and get a job.
>
> (Tracy, 46 years)

Indeed, for parents in particular, changes to conditions around eligibility for Australia's parenting support social security payments (Parenting Payment single and partnered), referred to by Tracy above and described earlier in Chapter 2, have increased economic stress and made the need for UBI even more pressing. Terri (30 years) noted, for example, that:

> When it was changed, the age of [eligibility for] single parent payments as well, just for example, I have friends who we have to help them buy groceries and stuff [now] because of that change. And they've ... got high needs kids...

Tracy (46 years) also described the harm of engaging with her disability employment services provider, who did not "actually have... any understanding of disability". For instance, one consultant told her she was "putting up barriers" to finding work. She responded, "No I'm not. My disability is putting up barriers" (Tracy, 46 years). Elsewhere, it has also been found that Australian employment services can be culturally incompetent and thereby be unsafe for First Nations peoples (e.g., Staines, 2018, 2021). For Pat (52 years), UBI would simply mean "not having to worry about all that bureaucracy" associated with Centrelink payments and thus also avoid associated stigma, which was also described by many as a significant cause of harm. I return to this issue of social-security related stigma, and related health and well-being effects, in Chapter 5.

Conclusion

As indicated at the outset of this chapter, women interviewees thought that, overall, their economic security would increase with the hypothetical UBI explored in this research. Indeed, a UBI could provide a crucial baseline of economic security, addressing (to some extent) the current gender pay gap and the inadequacies of the social security system. UBI could, for instance, help recognise and remunerate the disproportionate amount of unpaid care work undertaken by women. However, whether a UBI set at the rate explored here would meet the threshold of being sufficient to "provide a foundation of economic security for those whose care responsibilities might, at least for a time, preclude paid employment" is questionable and requires further consideration (Miller et al., 2023, p. 192). Additionally, UBI could enable women to make different choices about paid work, potentially assisting them to escape low-paid, precarious, or discriminatory employment.

There is also a risk that, for some women, a UBI might encourage them to reduce paid work to attend to caregiving, with possible negative consequences for long-term financial security. This is only a possible consequence of UBI, however, because of the unequal valuing of care labour under patriarchal forms of capitalism in the first place. Indeed, further work is needed to "demystify" the wage system along gendered lines (Weeks, 2011), and to correct the incredible devaluing of care that contributes not only to women's economic insecurity, but also to the "caring insecurity" experienced by other genders (Cook, 2019), and poorer societal well being overall (Fraser, 2016). Ultimately, a UBI alone cannot solve the deep-seated gender norms that lead to these disparities.

Overall, the findings of this chapter demonstrate the complex relationship between women's economic (in)security and UBI. In doing so, it sets the stage for Chapter 4, which considers more deeply the issue of violence against women. There, I expand on some of the themes introduced in this chapter—including how the social security system contributes to women's economic insecurity and exposure to violence. I also introduce new themes that arose in women's stories, including those related to maintaining safe homes and neighbourhoods. Again, the relationships between UBI and outcomes for women are complex, reinforcing that UBI is not a panacea to social issues affecting women. It may, however, provide much-needed extra support.

Notes

1 Australia became a signatory to the *International Covenant on Economic, Social and Cultural Rights* (1966) in 1972 and ratified it in 1975. Australia became a signatory to the *Convention on the Elimination of All Forms of Discrimination Against Women* (1979) in 1980 and ratified it in 1983.
2 This term was coined during a speech by former US President Ronald Reagan in 1976 (Cammett, 2014).
3 As described earlier in this Report, in 2006, mutual obligations were applied to those receiving Parenting Payments who had children under 16 and then, from 2013, to those with children under eight (Sobeck & Breunig, 2023).

4 Violence against women

> [UBI would provide] a greater level of autonomy, agency, and safety because it enables financial security that isn't tied to a partner... I know a lot of women who are in relationships and marriages that perhaps they wouldn't be in, or they definitely wouldn't be in, if they were financially independent.
>
> (Jules, 30 years)

It is estimated that about one third of all women across the world have experienced either physical or sexual violence at some point in their lives (World Health Organization, 2024). This excludes the millions of others who will also experience non-physical forms of violence, such as coercive control and economic abuse. However, notwithstanding global campaigns to end this violence as well as long-standing dedicated efforts across many countries to invest in domestic violence support services for all genders, the phenomenon is not waning.

In Australia, the Australian Bureau of Statistics' 2021–2022 Personal Safety Survey indicates that, since the age of 15, at least 17% of Australian women had experienced physical and/or sexual violence from a partner, 23% had experienced emotional abuse, and 16% had experienced economic abuse (AIHW, 2023). Amongst those who reported domestic violence, 30% had temporarily left the violent partner at least once, but later returned (Summers, 2022). Of those who returned, around 15% did so because they "had no money or nowhere else to go", with some stating that "Returning to their violent partner seemed a better choice than being homeless or trying to subsist in poverty" (Summers, 2022, p. 10). Overall, amongst the 70% of women who remained in violent relationships, about 47% expressed a desire to leave but cited "lack of money and financial support" as the main barrier (Summers, 2022, p. 10).

In addition to being financially devastating, leaving a violent partner can be extremely dangerous, with violence often escalating in the immediate aftermath (Our Watch, 2025; Summers, 2022). On average, one Australian woman is murdered every nine days by a current or former

DOI: 10.4324/9781003586593-4

partner, with the risk of homicide increasing after separation (Our Watch, 2025). In 2021–2022, an average of 15 women per day were hospitalised due to family and domestic violence (Our Watch, 2025). These risks are even more severe for women who face intersecting forms of social and economic marginalisation, including First Nations women, migrant women, and women with disabilities (McQuire, 2018). First Nations women, in particular, are eight times more likely than non-Indigenous women to be victims of intimate partner homicide (Cripps, 2023; McQuire et al., 2023) and 31 times more likely to be hospitalized as a result of domestic violence (Our Watch 2025). As McQuire (2018) states, for First Nations women, violence is "not just used as a tool of patriarchy—it was and is used as a tool of colonialism".

Violence was a recurring theme in the stories shared by the 26 women interviewed for this book. They spoke about how it shaped nearly every aspect of their lives—within their homes, intimate relationships, friendships, workplaces, and interactions with government services. Indeed, the ways that women talked about violence were broad, reflecting an acute awareness of how their experiences were shaped by intersecting systems of oppression, including patriarchy, colonialism, neoliberalism, and extractive capitalism. These overlapping forces were deeply embedded in their daily lives, and many women described the constant "bargaining" and negotiation required to survive within these constraints (Kandiyoti, 1988). Within this context, UBI was frequently discussed as one potential—though not singular—means of improving women's power in the face of these multiple oppressions.

This chapter explores two main ways women discussed UBI in relation to violence. First, I examine women's perspectives on how UBI might help them escape domestic and family violence. In this context, having an income independent of a partner—as Jules (30 years) mentions in the quote at the start of this chapter—is crucial. The unconditional nature of UBI is also significant, as it contrasts with other financial support options for women, such as social security benefits and one-off "ending violence payments". These alternatives are often highly conditional, making it difficult for many women to prove or maintain eligibility, which can itself be experienced as a form of violence (as touched on in Chapter 3). Second, I explore how UBI might help women avoid insecure and unsafe housing, which can also increase their vulnerability to violence.

Although I discuss these two themes separately, they are deeply interrelated. For example, finding stable housing that is affordable on a single income is often an important step for *escaping* domestic violence. And moreover, this is inflected by Australia's increasingly targeted and miserly social security system, as well as the nation's poor recent record at investing in social housing. Women spoke about how these (and other) forces combine to create a broader system of structural violence from which it is difficult to escape. Thus, while women's stories suggest that UBI could play a role as part of a broader framework for improving women's chances of escaping violence, it is not a complete solution. Much more work is needed to identify, unravel, and address the interlocking structures and systems that combine to oppress women, and which stand in their way when they attempt to escape situations of violence.

Escaping domestic and family violence

The decision to leave a family and domestic violence situation is deeply complex and influenced by myriad factors. Amongst others, such influences can include a desire to invest in and keep families together while protecting/shielding children from a breakup, and/or poor and re-victimising responses by criminal justice actors (Heron et al., 2020; Maher et al., 2021; Meyer, 2011, 2012). "Entrapment" can also be a key factor, whereby economic dependence, and physical and social isolation means women are unable to leave even if they wish to (Heron et al., 2020; Meyer, 2012). Indeed, the notion that women stay in violent relationships because they are financially trapped is widely documented in the research literature (e.g., Conner, 2014; Cortis & Bullen, 2016; Singh, 2020; Ulmestig & Eriksson, 2016) and was raised repeatedly by the women interviewed for this book. This situation is, of course, related to broader social structures that lead to women having disproportionately lower access to economic resources in the first place, as discussed in earlier chapters. Many of the women interviewed here spoke about finding themselves in such positions, and/or worrying about the risks posed by having to depend on others. For Terri (30 years), this is a primary reason for her deep concern about losing her income. As she saw it, "that's when domestic violence starts" (Terri, 30 years). For Tarnia (34 years), this was also the case in a previous marriage.

Tarnia (34 years) is a mother and, since leaving her marriage, has now also become a healthcare provider. Tarnia's former husband treated her as, in her words, "his possession" whereby she "couldn't do certain things" and "wasn't allowed to talk back". As she explained, "it escalated quite heavily to the point where I'm just like, 'Actually, I think I'm going to stay here and I'm going to die'". While Tarnia's story involved multiple incidents of violence, she spoke in the greatest detail about a traumatic ordeal during which her then-husband, wielding a knife, violently threatened to kill her and her (then) young child. Tarnia explained:

> ... I couldn't get out [of the house] and I'm like, "fuck, I'm probably going to die, actually". And then I'm like, "Actually, I don't fucking care, I'm too tired". And I actually, that thought went through my

> head. "If he kills me, well, at least I can sleep". And then my kid cried and then I'm just going, "fuck, that's right". Because I actually forgot she was behind me and he's coming at me [with a knife] and I'm like... "Okay, then. Well, we're going to get... Well, we've been hurt before. It's fine. We're good at this".

Tarnia went on to explain that her husband then inexplicably took a step backwards, during which she picked up her child and, while "shielding her", walked out of the room. As she described it, this was:

> ... the most confidence I probably ever had in my life because I'm like, "Well, he's going to kill me anyway. He probably won't kill the kid, but if he comes at me, I may as well be a sassy little bitch about it ..." This is a seven-year relationship at this point, where I've been fucked on my entire life. I can say it now, quite sadly, but at the time I was so beaten down. I felt like I was stuck in this big cloud that I couldn't... That no one else could see...

At this point, Tarnia was not able to leave due to fear of reprisal and because of a lack of financial resources. Moreover, it wasn't possible to turn to others for assistance because her abuser had isolated her from those who might be able to help. Those allowed into the family's sphere were only her husband's close and loyal friends:

> And they'd be like... "Oh, he's a good bloke. He's such a great guy". And I had no mates at that time because [I'd] kind of been separated from them all. It was just him and me and his mates who all loved him...

Ultimately, Tarnia did disclose her abuser's violence to an acquaintance, who assisted Tarnia and her child to leave the family home. This resulted in them spending the next three weeks homeless, sleeping on various acquaintances couches before eventually being taken in by a family member. They had minimal food available to them for at least six weeks after leaving, because basic needs such as this were simply unaffordable. During this time Tarnia "barely ate", making sure that any food she was able to find or afford went to her child.

On reflection, Tarnia explained that with a UBI she "would've left years earlier... and then just gone to... the other side of the fucking country". That is, a UBI would have enabled her to afford a means of escape, alternative accommodation, and sustenance: things she could not access as someone working in, at that time, a low-paid profession while simultaneously managing tertiary study and care of her child. Tarnia also reflected on how a UBI might have helped her own mother to leave what was a violent relationship with Tarnia's father much earlier, but also her grandmother before that:

> Well, on average, it takes seven tries to leave someone. You leave seven times. My mom, I think, did four. I did two. My grandma would've done fucking 10 ...

More than just assisting women to *leave*, however, Tarnia framed a UBI as having potential to "literally save lives". Now, working in the medical field, she regularly comes across victims of domestic violence, some of whom do not survive their injuries:

> I've seen women die from this [in my work]... I've done CPR on them. And it [UBI] would've saved them... I'm really sick of doing CPR on people who have been beaten to death by their husbands... I'm really sick of children coming in, because the ambos [ambulances] have to bring them in with their dead mothers, and watching me try and keep their mothers alive, and then the social worker leading them away... This [UBI] payment would've been truly lifesaving...

Similarly, Pat (52 years), who experienced domestic violence as a child, reflected that her:

> ...mother stayed in an abusive relationship for 25 years and endured enormous amounts of violence which she could have left a lot earlier if she'd had a guaranteed income... She would have been a single mum if she could have afforded it... It's had a devastating [impact] on not only her but also her three children.

Like Tarnia, Pat saw UBI as a means of enabling women, such as her mother, to escape violence earlier, and thereby reduce or avoid its intergenerational impacts. Erica (65 years) put it bluntly: "A basic income would ... give a woman an ... out from a relationship; she could plan how to get out".

In lieu of a UBI, Australia's social security system is meant to provide a safety net to which those experiencing poverty, including women escaping violence, can turn for support. However, as discussed in Chapter 3, it is often the case that the system itself is experienced as violent and harmful—something disproportionately encountered by women because their relative economic insecurity means they are more likely to be exposed to it in the first place (ACOSS, 2021; Staines et al. 2024). After leaving her violent husband, Tarnia (34 years) "refused to go" to enquire about social security payments because of her previous experiences of stigma and psychological harm in engaging with the system: a story that is not uncommon. More than this, though, Australian social security policies also create circumstances that can *further* erode women's independence. An example is Australia's enduring "couple rule", also touched on in Chapter 2.

Under the couple rule, the state treats a cohabiting couple as a united financial unit for the purpose of calculating income tax, but also for determining eligibility for government subsidies and payments, including social security. This, however, assumes that incomes and assets are shared fairly between partners, which fails to consider power dynamics *within* relationships that may govern women's reduced access to financial resources (Sleep, 2019, 2023; also Bick & Fuchs-Schündeln, 2017). It ignores, for instance, cases of economic violence and coercive control, where an abuser maintains control over financial resources as *part* of their violence (Cortis & Bullen, 2016; Singh, 2020). As Bindi (31 years) saw it, for women receiving social security, the couple rule *exacerbates* financial dependency on partners, limiting women's freedom to escape. Holly (27 years) talked about her own experience of the couple rule, reflecting on how "Because of my partner's income, my [social security] payments were reduced to $90 a fortnight". Holly, who also lives with disability, had a partner at the time who was abusive towards her but, she explained:

> I had no money... That's [$90 per fortnight] all I had to live on. There's not really any room there for squirrelling anything away to leave... I am terrified of losing that financial independence again... The thought of not being able to get out if I need to is distressing.

Holly eventually managed to escape the relationship through the support of close friends but explained that for women in similar situations,

> being able to have an income [such as UBI] that is paid to them, whether they are with their partner or not, being able to have their own money, I think that would change a lot of women's lives for the better.
>
> (Holly, 27 years)

This sentiment was reflected across nearly all interviews, for women on social security, but also for those with wage incomes, who were subjected to abuse by their partners (present or past).

Nevertheless, even though a UBI would also be paid to each person individually, women must also be able to maintain control over it. As Kiah (39 years) drew attention to, there is potential that, particularly for women in violent relationships, the "financial abuser is [the one] controlling [the UBI payment]". Such a situation was described by Casey (47 years):

> ...when I had one subject [of my tertiary studies] to go, and I had to pay for the other half of the course, he [former partner] wouldn't let me do that...We had a joint bank account [and] he transferred all the money out of the bank account into his own bank account in the middle of the night, and I was suddenly penniless... I had no money to fall back on until I would be paid again two weeks later.

While Kiah (39 years) suggested a need for avenues of recourse if a UBI were introduced, where a victim could swiftly redirect their UBI payments to an independent (and possibly secret) account when leaving a violent partner, there are ultimately no technical "fixes" that can completely solve this issue. This speaks, of course, to the need to address the root causes of violence in the first place. A UBI might offset at least some of the economic costs of escaping violence, which can plunge victims into situations of dire economic insecurity, often leaving them with a grotesque choice between enduring violence or living in dire poverty (Summers, 2022). However, it has limited ability to drastically augment the wider social and economic conditions that disproportionately place women at higher risk of violence to begin with, as I return to later.

Aside from Australia's highly conditional social security system, and ad hoc support available from the charitable sector (which varies in availability and quality, including between urban, regional, and remote locations), Australian women have few other places to turn for economic support to leave violent relationships. In an effort to remedy this, the Australian Government established a two-year pilot "Escaping Violence Payment" (EVP) in October 2021, which is administered by third-sector provider UnitingCare and provides emergency access to up to $5,000 in funding (i.e., up to $1,500 cash and $3,500 in non-cash goods, services, and support) to victims of domestic and family violence to "reduce... financial barriers associated with leaving" (DSS, 2023b, p. 3). Nearly two years into the pilot, 89% of the 19,000 people who had accessed the program were women, while 28% of these individuals also identified as Indigenous (DSS, 2023b, p. 4).

A recent evaluation reported overall program satisfaction, but also several challenges with program consultation, design, implementation, length, and sufficiency. Moreover, between July–September 2023, more than half of those applying for the EVP were rejected, having been deemed ineligible for varied reasons, including not having the right documentation such as doctor's reports, or being unable to demonstrate financial hardship as they did not have a bank account in their name (Kelly, 2024). This indicates the program is designed to fundamentally mistrust those who seek these payments (primarily women), placing onus on them to turn to others (e.g., medical staff) to substantiate their claims of victimisation *before* they can access financial support. However, accessing medical professionals is often prohibitively expensive for women on low incomes (as I expand on in Chapter 5) (Branley & Thorne, 2024), and even more so in remote locations where there are far fewer services available. Moreover, not having an account in one's own name can also be a *symptom* of violence.

This (and other) conditions placed on the EVP are considerable hurdles for applicants who are otherwise focused on simple survival. In a country where domestic, family, and sexual violence remains rife, it seems obvious that EVPs should at the very least be provided in an immediate and urgent manner, enabling the claims of those seeking support to be taken as *prima facie* truth. If accountability checks are to be undertaken, these should be post hoc to avoid victims being unable to access independent payments at the time they are most urgently needed. Ultimately, however, this again draws attention to the administrative simplicity of a UBI, whereby women would not be at risk of being deemed ineligible for independent financial support. Again, a UBI is not only promising for its ability to provide an avenue of independent financial support to women but also because it would do so on a basis of trust, rather than prohibitive conditions.

Escaping insecure and unsafe housing

In addition to providing an avenue for improving women's freedom from domestic and family violence, UBI has also been proposed as one means, amongst a broader suite of measures, that can contribute to addressing homelessness and housing insecurity—both of which also increase women's risk of experiencing violence (e.g., Clarke, 2023; Kerman, 2021). For older Australian women, rates of homelessness increased by more than 30% between 2011 and 2016 (AHRC, 2019), stabilising at around 19 out of every 10,000 women aged 55+ years by the 2021 Census (AHURI, 2021). This is due to a multitude of complex factors (e.g., Darab & Hartman, 2013) but includes changes to Australian social policies, including some described earlier, that have exacerbated gender inequalities (e.g., see Smith, 2017; Stewart, 2017).[1] Moreover, it again includes the long-term impacts of devaluing women in the economy, which results in Australian women having around 38.8% less superannuation to support them in their retirement years when compared with men (WGEA, n.d.).

This alarming situation was referred to several times by interviewees and shaped many women's worries about the future. For Jana (44 years), securing safe and stable housing was a primary, overriding concern:

> ...that's such a big issue, homelessness, and especially with elder single women. So yeah, that's a big worry of mine is what's going to happen in the future. [I] don't have money to fall back on.

Similarly, Eva (58 years) spoke about how having a UBI would provide "just that assurance as you face the future that you're not going to be homeless..." Alex (63 years), who described herself as "nearing retirement age" was lucky to receive a property as part of an unexpected inheritance, without which she explained, "I was looking down the barrel of being homeless in five years' time". Alex's single-parent status meant that, over her lifetime, she had not been able to accumulate sufficient wealth, including superannuation, to support her post-retirement housing needs. In lieu of this inheritance, a UBI would have provided an alternative lifeline to avoid her becoming homeless.

Tam (55 years), who did not have a similar inheritance safety net, *had* previously experienced homelessness, having to "couch-surf for about six months" due to an inability to afford rent. She described this as an incredibly difficult situation that "eats away at you, your sense of positivity, your mental bandwidth". In contrast, she said a UBI "would be... like instead of feeling like you're running on quicksand, I'd feel like I had a platform to run on" (Tam, 55 years). UBI would also help reduce barriers to seeking support, which thrust some women into homelessness. Erica (65 years), for example, described how an acquaintance had become homeless because she did not wish to engage with the stigmatising social security system:

> She is homeless. [But] she really believes that she shouldn't be getting government handout[s]. So if there was a government handout to everybody [in the form of UBI] she would just say, "Oh yeah, that's my normal UBI", [and] she wouldn't be living on the streets... There wouldn't be shame in getting [that UBI] government handout.

More than just providing support for older women, though, UBI was also discussed as one means of increasing the availability of safer housing options for women of *all ages*, and in diverse circumstances. For parents of children, for instance, not having access to safe and stable housing can draw the attention of government child services. As someone who experienced living in state care herself as a child, Emma (33 years) explained that:

> ... the housing crisis [is] pushing a lot of kids into foster care because people can't afford accommodation... and [with UBI] maybe people would stop being punished simply for being born, for daring to be born with parents who don't have any resources.

The housing crisis that Emma refers to is ongoing in Australia and has culminated from decades of policy (in)action, which has created conditions of high demand and low supply in both the purchase and rental markets, alongside longer-term underinvestment in social housing (Azize, 2023; Dufty-Jones, 2017). Indeed, over the last 40 years, Australia's social housing has fallen from ~4.9% to 3.8% of overall stock (AHURI, 2022). This compares poorly with the proportion of social housing stock in international jurisdictions, such as Aotearoa/New Zealand (4%), Canada (4.2%), Ireland (9%), France (16%), Scotland (24%), and the Netherlands (29.1%) (AHURI, 2022). Moreover, even those deemed eligible for Australian social housing face excruciatingly long waiting lists (Morris, 2023). For example, in the state of New South Wales, people can wait ten or more years for social housing, which frustrates efforts to flee violence but can also be experienced as violent in and of itself (Morris, 2023). As one female participant in Morris' (2023) study put it, "Running from him [an abusive ex-partner] was hard enough but asking them [the housing department] for help is ten times worse" (also see Morris et al., 2022).

For women on low incomes but who are not eligible for social housing, or who are left to languish on long waiting lists, private rented share houses are often the next most affordable option, with some interviewees describing themselves as "dependent on living in share houses with others on the lease" because of their low incomes and lack of accumulated wealth (Pat, 52 years). For many, having to live in share house accommodation had, however, exposed them to unsafe and sometimes violent situations, which could have been avoided if they could afford safer housing. For example, Jules (30 years) explained:

> I did the share house thing for probably eight or nine years. In multiple instances, someone would invite someone over without asking everyone else, and there would be a very intimidating or kind of violent person. But the worst one was when I first moved to [name of city]... There was a much older woman... and her son... and they were both drug affected... And they were just really intimidating, kind of scary people to live with.

> And the guy in particular, he had no boundaries. So if I would walk out of the bathroom after having a shower, he would try and follow me to my room. Or kind of corner me in the kitchen… Or one night when he cornered me in the kitchen, he randomly just pulled up his shirt and showed me he had a bunch of stab wounds… So just really inappropriate, scary behaviour that made me feel unsafe… So even though the door did lock [in] my bedroom, I didn't feel safe because I thought, "Well, if he really wants to get in, he could". So, I moved out not long after that and I didn't get my bond back because the real estate agent said that I had broken the [lease] contract, but he was kind of just lying because he said that it was a short month to month thing, so it wasn't locked in… But yeah, I think having that [basic] income to live by yourself, especially as a young woman is, that's literally life changing to live safely…

These kinds of situations are similarly reflected in other studies (e.g., Darab et al., 2018), whereby share houses have been described as greatly reducing women's privacy, autonomy, and safety. As one participant in Darab et al.'s (2018, p. 533) study put it, "I'd rather live in a tent on my own than a share house". Nevertheless, although UBI would improve the amount of income available to cover the costs associated with safe housing, it would fail to address "supply" side issues (Clarke, 2023). Ultimately, as Clarke (2023, p. 862, emphasis added) explains, the ability of a UBI to address unsafe housing or homelessness depends "on whether it is coupled with other universalist measures, like increased social housing and rent control, that address the cost *and* supply side of the problem". Again, while a UBI would very likely assist, it is just one approach in what needs to be a larger toolkit.

Conclusion

As I write this chapter, protests have again been occurring across Australia, calling for more serious action to put a stop to violence against women. This has arisen in the wake of the shocking fact that on average, one woman was killed in Australia every four days in 2024, prompting the Australian Prime Minister to declare this issue a "national emergency" (Watson & Ritchie, 2024). Just one week after these protests, however, the nation's media turned its attention to an incident at a prestigious private school in the Yarra Valley (Victoria), where a group of Year 11 boys were caught sharing a spreadsheet on social media that rated their female peers according to how "rape-able" they were (ABC News, 2024). Two of the boys were expelled and there has been national outrage, with Victoria's state premier Jacinta

Allan also weighing in to express her condemnation (ABC News, 2024; Kelly, 2024).

Meanwhile, the latest data on national attitudes towards violence against women (Coumarelos et al., 2023a) indicates that nearly half of 1,669 young Australians (16–24 years) surveyed do not understand the gendered nature of domestic violence and that many still hold problematic views. For instance, 26% of respondents believe that women who stay with abusive partners are to blame for their victimisation, 30% agree that women exaggerate their claims of domestic violence, and 21% agree that in rape cases, "a lot of times" the woman had "led the man on" (Coumarelos et al., 2023a). Other data, surveying 19,100 Australian adults (16+ years) on similar attitudes show disturbingly comparable results; although attitudes are very slowly improving across the board, there is a long way to go before this engrained sexism is overcome (Coumarelos et al., 2023b). Moreover, as discussed throughout this chapter, these attitudes are precipitated and reinforced by broader social structures that devalue women and create contexts that increase women's likelihood of experiencing violence. It is unsurprising, therefore, that the overall pace of change is slow.

Drawing on earlier work by Walby (2009), Hearn et al. (2022) discuss how "violence regimes" can mean that violence itself becomes a central and intended regulating concept, working across all domains of society (economy, polity and more) and at all levels (micro, meso, macro). In this conceptualisation, violence takes many forms:

> Direct physical violence is not always necessary, especially following earlier violence or threat or existence of structural violence and power imbalance, as in slavery, colonialism, imperialism, capitalism, and patriarchy.
>
> (Hearn et al., 2022, p. 699)

The social-ecological model of violence also bears this out, suggesting that long-term solutions will see us acting across multiple levels (individual, relationship, community, societal) concurrently (Dahlberg & Krug, 2002, p. 13; Our Watch, 2025). This concept of violence as a broader regime is deeply apparent in this chapter. It is not sufficient to consider violence against women as only involving acts by single individuals. Instead, and as women in this study recognised, individual expressions of violence have their roots in broader hegemonic structures that uphold violent masculinities while subjugating women (e.g., Flood, 2019; Garcia, 2021). Gender-based violence is, for instance, also embedded in and perpetuated in overlapping ways by other major social institutions, including Australia's social security system, housing system, and the economy more broadly, in its continued structural devaluing of women's labour. In this respect, and as the women cited in this chapter speak to, UBI is not a panacea for ending violence against women. In Terri's (30 years) view, however, it would be a way of going *beyond* awareness raising alone:

> Yeah, I just think a lot of programs that exist to empower women or prevention of domestic violence, it's all this ... awareness raising stuff. Where it's like... "This is a red flag if your partner's this way". And it's like, well, women aren't stupid, they know, but there are actual barriers in place for them taking action when they notice these things... And I think a big part of that is this financial insecurity, especially if there are kids in the picture. And I think UBI is such a functional way to support women to make those choices instead of just continuously doing this awareness raising.
>
> (Terri, 30 years)

UBI cannot alone solve violence against women. However, as one tool in a broader package of strategies, it holds serious potential to assist them to take stronger and quicker action to halt and escape the violence they encounter. As I turn to the next chapter, this is just one of the ways that UBI might also help improve women's longer-term health and well-being.

Note

1 An example is, for instance, changes to eligibility around age pension and superannuation, meaning "women are now ineligible for the aged pension until aged 65 but generous superannuation is available to many men from 55 years" (Smith, 2017, p. 183).

5 Women's health

> I know some friends who do constantly struggle [financially] and it affects their mental health a lot, their mental health and wellbeing... [and their] physical health over time... But, if you knew that there is this set amount of money coming in, and you're not under any obligations as to how you're going to get that money, or how you're going to spend it, I think that would be really reassuring. I can imagine that would be really reassuring.
>
> (Chandra, 33 years)

Sex plays a key role in health outcomes. On average, men have shorter lifespans than women and are more likely to suffer from chronic heart disease and road injuries (Patwardhan et al., 2024). Women tend to live longer but experience higher rates of poor mental health, such as anxiety and depression, as well as conditions like arthritis, osteoporosis, and chronic pain (Patwardhan et al., 2024). In Australia, these trends hold true. About a quarter of Australian women aged 15+ years have long-term mental illnesses, while nearly one in five experience chronic back problems (AIHW, 2023a, 2023b, 2024b). Pregnancy and childbirth can also have serious health effects, and research shows that mothers often experience a decline in psychological well-being over time, whereas women without children tend to have more stable mental health (Kuipers et al., 2021; Vogel et al., 2024). Owing to ongoing colonialism and engrained structural racism, First Nations peoples also experience poorer overall health across the life course and lower life expectancies—75.6 years for First Nations women, compared with 85.1 years for non-Indigenous women (ABS, 2024a, 2024c; AIHW, 2024a, 2024b, 2024c; Dudgeon & Walker, 2015).

Economic security is a key social determinant of health (Ruckert et al., 2018, p. 3). In Australia, economic *in*security has been associated with worse physical and mental health (Kendall et al., 2019; Muthalaly et al., 2023; Rohde et al., 2016, 2017), while poorer mental health also often *reinforces* economic insecurity (e.g., through job loss, lower productivity,

DOI: 10.4324/9781003586593-5

and more) (Ridley et al., 2020). Research highlights the need for "upstream" interventions to strengthen economic security and improve health outcomes (Muthalaly et al., 2023). Since income is "widely considered to be the most important social determinant of health", some argue that UBI could help reduce long-term health inequities (Ruckert et al., 2018, p. 3).

Globally, UBI programs have shown improved outcomes for child health, mental well-being, and access to healthcare, while also improving education and housing security—both crucial for better health, as touched on in the previous chapter (Johnson et al., 2022; Ruckert et al., 2018). Johnson et al. (2022) identify three key pathways via which a UBI can impact health: reducing resource scarcity, alleviating chronic stress, and enabling long-term planning rather than short-term survival. Using these pathways as a framework, this chapter explores how women perceive UBI's potential benefits for their own health and that of their families and communities.

First, I canvass the potential impacts of UBI on reducing resource scarcity and affecting subsequent behaviours. For many of the women interviewed, including those with disabilities (and/or who have dependents with disabilities), UBI would improve access to healthy foods, medical needs, and other essential supports: key factors for maintaining good health. Second, I examine UBI's potential to reduce chronic stress, a major theme in women's stories (Johnson et al., 2021). Economic stability from UBI could ease stress linked to financial hardship, but women also highlighted how it could reduce the stigma and isolation of poverty. This includes the stress of having to engage with Australia's demeaning social security system.

While the stories summarised in this chapter offer further support for UBI, they again reinforce that it is not a cure-all for the shortcomings of other health-related systems and services, including Australia's Medicare system and National Disability Insurance Scheme (NDIS). Indeed, although women repeatedly indicated that UBI would be a helpful supplement to existing health and social services, their stories also reveal deep issues with these existing supports that a UBI cannot fix.

UBI, resource scarcity, and health behaviours

Johnson et al. (2021, p. 410) claim that, because "UBI increases resources and reduces absolute poverty, there is potential for improvements in material capacity for promotion of health". This was a common theme in women's stories about how a UBI might impact them and those around them—some of which connect closely with the topics canvassed in Chapter 3. Indeed, women repeatedly talked about how a UBI would provide access to basic needs that had otherwise been limited at one or more points in their lives, including food, clothing, shelter, and healthcare (Chiappero-Martinetti, 2014). For some who'd had extreme experiences of food insecurity, UBI would improve the ability to access good quality, healthy food that would support their well-being. As Tam (55 years) explained:

> Sometimes I couldn't afford to eat properly or eat much. So after a few days of not eating, you start to shake and get physically weak. So I couldn't even go for a walk because of being too weak… [UBI] would've completely transformed the situation.

Across Australia in 2024, roughly 3.4 million households (~32% of all households) experienced food insecurity, with lack of affordability being a primary cause (FoodBank Australia, 2024). In 2015–2016, ~80% of all Australian households that reported food insecurity were receiving some form of social security payment (Temple et al., 2019), and the situation is also worse for those in remote parts of Australia, with costs of food being far higher, particularly in remote First Nations communities (Staines & Smith, 2022). Overall, women are more likely to be food insecure than men; particularly single mothers and survivors of domestic and family violence (Paterson & Farrugia, 2020). For instance, after escaping domestic violence, Tarnia (34 years) couch-surfed with her daughter—a story detailed in Chapter 4. During this time, she "barely ate for six weeks" to ensure her daughter "never went without food". Later, when she could afford it, Tarnia occasionally treated her daughter to a takeaway meal, but this often meant going without food herself the next day. Fighting back tears, Tarnia explained that a UBI:

> … would mean the world back then… Oh honestly, it's so hard. Because that's all you want, isn't it? I mean, really, you just want your kids to be okay. You want them to be better. You want them to have more opportunities than you have, and you just want them not to have to do what you had to do.

For Pat (52 years), the food she buys on her current social security payment "has to be reasonably cheap", meaning she tends to purchase foods that are not necessarily best for her health. With a UBI, she explained, she would be able to "eat better" to manage her autoimmune diagnoses.

> I would buy more organic food and grow more of my own and also eat more protein, fish, that tends to be expensive (Pat, 52 years).

On her current income, Pat shares a rental house with others, which is "damp and mouldy… It's cheap but it's crap". With a UBI, Pat reflected that she may be able to afford to live elsewhere, in a location and environment that better supported her health. She would also be able to "have more psychology sessions, go to yoga… see a dentist", as well as have long-awaited surgery on her broken nose, which would help her sleep and give her "more energy".

Putting off healthcare needs because of unaffordability is something that many other women also raised. It is also something that is recognised as a growing issue in Australia more broadly (Méndez et al., 2022). For instance, Angeles et al. (2023, p. 323) reported that overall, "About 30% of chronic disease in Australia is considered preventable, but only 1.8% of health care spending is for preventative interventions". Relatedly, Hannah (42 years) described how she believes she has another "encroaching health issue" that she cannot afford to have diagnosed because doing so would mean a pathway to "more appointments, more tests… more money". With a UBI she said she would "address health issues earlier on", giving her "peace of mind" and potentially improving her longer-term well-being. Similarly, Indigenous woman Zayla (31 years) explained that access to a UBI in the past would have meant she would have had an earlier diagnosis of an existing health issue, leading to better long-term outcomes. While Australia performs well compared to other wealthy nations in health outcomes and spending (10.2% of GDP), overall access to care remains a challenge due to affordability and long wait times (Méndez et al., 2022).

Australia's universal health insurance system, "Medicare" (formerly "Medibank"[1]), gives all citizens (and some non-citizens) access to both free and subsidised basic health services, funded via a means-tested Medicare levy and Medicare levy surcharge, with the latter being applied to those who earn above a certain income level and/or those without a certain level of private hospital insurance (Services Australia, 2023a, 2023b, 2024a). Medicare is also supported by Australia's Pharmaceutical Benefits Scheme (PBS), which provides subsidised access to medications listed and approved under the scheme. However, while Medicare and the PBS combine to cover or subsidise the costs of many basic healthcare and medication needs, they are not exhaustive, with several services and medications remaining unapproved/unlisted (Department of Health and Aged Care, 2025). Perhaps most notably, Medicare does not cover most dental services. Instead, these costs these are covered out-of-pocket by patients, making dental care often prohibitively expensive and remaining a source of long-standing debate in Australian politics (Clarke & Cutler, 2024). Alternatively, patients able to afford private health insurance can claim benefits related to dental services from their private provider, though the cost of private health means this is not an option for a large proportion of the Australian population, as I return to later (APRA, 2024).[2] This was the case for many women in this study, who either "put off… going to the dentist" because of the cost (Camille, 42 years), or simply weren't able to go at all, because they "just couldn't afford it" (Jana, 44 years). For Jana and her children, being able to afford to visit the dentist and attend to other health matters with a UBI might mean "we all wouldn't be as unwell as we are, because we'd get on top of things earlier". Similarly, Jules (30 years) considered going to the dentist to be a "luxury" that she simply could not afford.

In their narrative historical review of 76 published articles relating to Medicare from 2000 onwards, Angeles et al. (2023, p. 323) recently argued that, overall, the:

> …current financing structure reflects a complex and fragmented health care system that struggles to provide effective patient-centred care, patients experience a lack of integration, coordination, and continuity of care between sectors…. [While] Several models of integrated care have been tried in Australia… progress toward a national integrated system has been disappointing…

Access to inexpensive healthcare in Australia is also heavily dictated by location and availability, with the overall number of general practitioners (GPs) providing bulk-billed (fully subsidised) services declining over time and with far fewer services available in regional and remote areas (Méndez et al., 2022). As Alex (63 years) explained, "nobody bulk bills anymore; my GP charges $90 [per appointment]". Several women in this study also spoke about how accessing specialist diagnoses for neurodivergence for both themselves and/or their children had proven to be both complicated and prohibitively expensive, even after Medicare rebates were applied. Marley (35 years) explained:

> The pathways [to diagnosis] for adults are very limited and there's not much. If you go through, say, a psychiatrist, you get a little bit of Medicare back, but a lot of psychiatrists charge $800 for one session. If you go through a psychology clinic, you get nothing back from Medicare and you're looking at $2,000 plus. So, a lot of people just can't afford that kind of process.

Holly (27 years) had a similar experience:

> …I have a referral to [name of service], which is a clinic for [name of medical conditions] … The initial appointment is $400 out of pocket. That's more than I get for a week to live on. So, it's completely

> untenable for me at the moment to drop that kind of money on an initial appointment…
>
> (Holly, 27 years)

While this affects all Australians, Marley described how diagnoses of neurodivergence are particularly complicated for women:

> A lot of these people who struggle to get diagnoses are women just because of the, I guess, bias in the medical community anyway. So it's even harder for them to seek that support…

For Tarnia (34 years), this has also impacted her daughter, delaying a subsequent diagnosis of attention deficit hyperactivity disorder (ADHD), which ultimately paved the way to access appropriate support and treatment. This gender bias is substantiated in broader research, with higher rates of delayed diagnoses in women being associated with experiences of poorer mental health and significant distress (Castañeda, 2023; Riches & North, 2024). For instance, Tarnia, who herself was diagnosed as neurodivergent in adulthood, explained how securing this diagnosis earlier would have drastically changed her life course: "The incidences of children undiagnosed who actually come out of that with a drug or an alcohol habit or raging suicide, it's insane… I look back and [think about] the amount of times I nearly died". Terri (30 years) described how a delayed diagnosis also negatively impacted her own well-being:

> Yeah, so I have both ADHD and autism. And it's only now that I've been able to actually get that diagnosed and get proper treatment. And my quality of life has so improved. And it's because I married a rich guy, to be frank. That's the only reason. I have friends who are looking for diagnosis as well. And if their parents can't pay or their partner doesn't have money, then it just doesn't happen and they just don't get any support. And the impacts on that, the longer you delay treatment and support, the worse you get burnt out. Well with the disabilities I have. And then you just can't come back from that level of burnout once you get to a certain point.

Terri's story again underlines the link between economic security and access to essential health services—something she and others believe UBI could support. This is especially relevant in a policy environment that increasingly encourages citizens to purchase private health insurance to ease pressure on the public system (Angeles et al., 2023). This includes via a government rebate on private health insurance premiums, active since 1999, which has helped push private coverage levels back to nearly what they were before Medicare's introduction in 1984 (ABS, 2001). By 2023, 14.7 million Australians (~55%) had private insurance, most of whom are higher-income earners (Butler, 2024). This trend reinforces healthcare inequalities, as private patients face shorter wait times than those in the public system, where access is triaged according to urgency (Yang et al., 2024). For instance, a study in Victoria found that every 1% increase in private coverage reduces wait times by about 0.3 days (Yang et al., 2024). Alex (63 years) purchased private health insurance when she had her child, though affording it has been a challenge:

> ...it's always been a struggle. But when I had son, I got it because I didn't want ever to be in a situation where I couldn't [afford health care]. And it's a huge amount of money, but I've stuck to it and I've paid it. I've paid it when I've had to go without stuff. So yeah, [UBI] would help huge amounts [with that]...

Before purchasing insurance, Alex was on a public health waitlist for urgent sinus surgery for two years. After purchasing private insurance and waiting a further year (her health provider's exclusion period), she was able to finally have the operation. She reflected:

> So I can't imagine what people are like [waiting in the public system]. I know people who have got bad hips and stuff and can't do anything about it because they can't [afford private health]. Yeah... my mother has been on a waiting list for hip surgery [in the public system] for four years now.

This has occurred alongside broader trends that have seen widening inequalities in income and wealth reflected in growing health inequalities across Australia (Flavel et al., 2022). Ultimately, "socially disadvantaged Australians not only live shorter lives but ... their already-shorter lives are [also] more burdened with [limiting long-term illnesses]" (Xu & Payne, 2024, p. 243). This includes long-term poorer mental health, which is far higher for people living in poverty (Isaacs et al., 2018). For instance, research has indicated that about 25% of the poorest one-fifth of Australians report high or very high psychological distress, compared with only 10% of Australians in the richest quintile (Isaacs et al., 2018). On the topic of mental health, Jana (44 years) shared a devastating story of one of her children, who had died by suicide as a young adult. She explained:

> I think with the [UBI] income, it would've made a difference... [They] died [from] mental illness... if I'd been able to spend more time at home and not be working... it would've helped just to have

> some more time with [them]... you should be able to access all the things that you need... within the health system... Last year I was paying for myself to see a psychologist fortnightly and for [them] to see one weekly, and we didn't have money for other things at all. Every cent went on trying to help [them].

Jana's palpably tragic experience with her child reinforces the need to improve access to subsidised mental health supports, particularly for young people at risk of suicide (Hill et al., 2021). For young First Nations people, who are at an even disproportionately higher risk, programs and policies that maintain cultural connection are also crucially important (Dudgeon et al. 2021; Gibson et al., 2021). However, affordability and geographic remoteness remain the most significant barriers to Australians seeking mental health support (Corscadden et al., 2018; Meadows et al., 2015). For instance, individuals can only claim government Medicare rebates for up to 10 individual and 10 group sessions with a mental health professional per calendar year, meaning any remaining sessions must be paid for out of pocket (Services Australia, 2023a, 2023b). Even with rebated sessions, patients often still need to cover a significant "gap" cost.

The 2024–2025 Australian Psychological Society national schedule of suggested fees indicates that a standard consultation (~50–60 minutes) should be set at around $311 (APS, 2025). Meanwhile, the available Medicare rebate for a session of this length is only $141.85, leaving a gap of $169.15 for just one psychology session (Department of Health and Aged Care, 2025). Low- or no-cost options are also available via community health centres, though access to these is not universal and waitlists are, again, long (Petrie et al., 2021). Ultimately, this means that access to psychology services remains prohibitively expensive for many (Petrie et al., 2021). The costs of maintaining good health can be even higher for people with disabilities.

UBI and people with disability

In Australia, 21% of males and 21.8% of females live with a disability, with rates increasing sharply from age 55 onward (ABS, 2024b). Shania (31 years), who was previously employed but had to leave work due to her disability, now lives with a family member. She requires a shower chair, but due to the bathroom's design must lift the chair in and out of the shower every time she bathes, adding to the physical challenges she faces. For Shania,

> ... moving that chair is, on a bad day, enough to wipe out the ability for me to then actually have the shower... [and] as [an] outcome of that,

> I now keep my head shaved because I just can't keep my hair clean, so I just don't keep hair anymore… it's … frustrating because I know that I could manage it if I could live in a space that was appropriate.

This also affects women who are supporting children with special needs:

> My child recently got new leg splints. That means that they are further up their leg, which means I had to buy all new knee-high socks. And knee-high socks are very expensive… When you have a disabled child you can't buy basics like shoes, socks, from [a discount store]. You have to buy specific shoes that fit their splints and orthotics… All of those little things are more expensive…
>
> (Casey, 47 years)

Alongside Medicare and the PBS, Australia's NDIS, launched in July 2013, represents the country's first national program providing funding directly to individuals with permanent and significant disabilities. It has been described as a "bold and substantial reform", being the first of its kind globally (Dickinson & Yates, 2023, p. 461; DPM&C, 2023). However, like Medicare and the PBS, the NDIS leaves many costs uncovered. For instance, the special shoes and socks Casey referred to above "are not covered by the NDIS". Marley (35 years), who also has a child with disability, explained:

> We've attempted multiple times, but [my child] can't do group swimming lessons. So [they're] actually in a disability specific one where it's one on one, but NDIS doesn't like to cover swimming lessons because they deem it parental responsibility, so they don't like to cover a lot of things that they deem as parental responsibility. So if [they] didn't have a disability, [they] wouldn't be in the swimming class, but it's still my responsibility, so I've got to pay double what the general parent would pay. And some people do get it covered, but it's really hard. So there's a lot of grey area around that…

The NDIS has also been found to have several other significant limitations and is currently undergoing a "reset" (Carey et al., 2021; Dickinson & Yates, 2023; DPM&C, 2023). As a recent review found, "The quality of supports across NDIS markets are highly variable, and as the Disability Royal Commission concluded, sometimes lead to harm" with the "planning process [being described] as confusing and frustrating … [or] At worse… as traumatic" (DPM&C, 2023, pp. 26, 32). Some studies have also found that access to the NDIS is particularly challenging for women and girls, including due to gender discrimination in diagnoses and within the medical system more broadly—such as that described earlier in relation to neurodivergence (Yates et al., 2021). As women tend to be most likely to be caregivers, including for those with disability, they are also often the ones managing NDIS plans, which can be incredibly complicated and time-consuming, with "a lot of hoops to jump through" (Jana, 44 years). As Marley (35 years) noted, however, the NDIS doesn't "pay you for the time spent managing it all". Aside from eating into women's time, managing interactions with the health-care system can be incredibly stressful. This taps into another key theme that women's stories touched on: the possibility that a UBI might reduce chronic stress and thereby, positively impact mental health.

UBI and chronic stress

A significant and recurring theme in women's stories was that a UBI, by improving their economic security, would significantly reduce stress, anxiety, and general financial worry. Indeed, by supporting financial independence, a UBI was seen as potentially enabling women to build greater "self-confidence" and a "sense of self-worth" (Chandra, 33 years), improving their "power and the ability to undertake what they want … or need to do with their own wellbeing" (Erica, 65 years). The additional income provided by a UBI would enable, for instance, women to feel less "isolated", giving them "energy or time to participate" in social and civic activities (Terri, 30 years)—important for sustaining good mental health (Wang et al., 2017). Casey (47 years) explained that the income provided by a UBI would help address isolation in several ways:

> It's expensive to address that isolation, because you need to pay for a babysitter or you need to participate in social activities that cost money. You can't simply go to your friend's house to have coffee, because you don't have those friends anymore. And now that I can't work, that was really, largely, my social outlet, and I had a few good friends at work. Now that I'm not working, I don't have that. So if I wanted to socialise, I would need to participate in things that cost money, and possibly those things would occur outside of school hours, so I would need to pay for a babysitter, so access to a UBI would mean I'd be able to do that.

Tam (55 years) explained how, while living on a very low income as an unemployment benefit recipient, she felt "abandoned by society, anxious, depressed" and like she was in a "downward spiral". Tam explained that:

> …living on a very low income is bad for social connection and it brings on social isolation. And I did struggle with social isolation

> because I lost contact with friends. I couldn't even get on the tram to go and see them to have a cup of tea, for example. I got sick and tired of continually telling them I couldn't afford to see them. So that is hard… [Poverty] jolts you out of connection with your community.

When asked how a UBI might have changed things, Tam responded:

> Radically. Absolutely radically. It would've completely transformed the situation. It would've transformed my mental and emotional health. It would've transformed my personal social connections and it would've transformed my sense of place in the world, radically…

Having greater stability would relieve stress and improve mental health for not only women, but also for those around them. As Indigenous woman, Zayla (31 years) explained:

> It'll [UBI] help because a lot of… mental [ill] health is actually because of financial burden… When you start thinking how to pay bills, thinking of how to cater for yourself and your loved ones, it's a kind of stress. When you realise that your loved ones as well are receiving this basic income, it'll definitely reduce your financial burden and reduce your worries.

Others also said that a UBI would give them a stronger sense of belonging and deep gratitude. As Zayla (31 years) also put it, "This [would] become like a gift from the government… [that] the government is just giving you support to appreciate you as a citizen. There is a great joy in receiving a gesture…". Zayla went on to explain how receiving such a gift would make her want to "show gratitude to the government" by "giving back" through community service volunteering. Others, such as Keira (25 years), said they would do the same. For those on social security incomes, a UBI might enable them to avoid what they saw as the stigmatising effects of engaging with the social security system, as I also touched on in Chapter 3.

UBI and avoiding social security stigma

Camille (42 years) explained that a UBI would mean not having to "deal [as much]… with Centrelink" which "exacerbate[s]… mental health issues". For Emma (33 years), a UBI could mean "I might reach that point where I can come off the antidepressants". Speaking quietly so that her housemate, who is unaware that she receives social security payments, wouldn't hear, Pat (52 years) described how having a UBI would mean that she would no longer need to worry about experiencing the deep and hurtful "stigma" that accompanies the receipt of social security in Australia. A UBI would mean:

> ...not being cast into that, you're not worthy, and you're on benefits, that kind of thing and, for me personally, not having the shame and stigma of having to justify yourself all the time. Having to explain to people or make up stories.
>
> (Pat, 52 years)

This stigma is not only deeply harmful but also prevents some from accessing social security altogether. For instance, Tarnia (34 years) explained:

> After I left my (abusive) now ex-husband, and I was thinking "Well, I don't want to go back there" [to Centrelink]. I actually refused to go there... I didn't eat for like... I had minimal food for six weeks because I refused to go there [to Centrelink]... The stigma is [significant]... and it's so psychologically draining. I was like, "No, I can't fucking do that"... But that'd be really interesting, getting rid of that stigma by giving it [UBI] to everyone no matter what.

Casey (47 years) talked about what she saw as the absurdity of the public discourse around welfare receipt in Australia, which denigrates social security recipients, while ignoring others who receive alternative forms of state support such as Medicare and tax subsidies.

> If everybody got a UBI, I wonder whether that would improve that attitude in society, whether the feeling that someone is getting an advantage would be taken [away]. And also, I think society doesn't recognise that everybody receives welfare. So the person on JobSeeker receives a welfare payment, but the person who is working fulltime and gets Childcare Subsidy is also receiving a welfare payment. And the person when they go to hospital and use Medicare, they're getting welfare... There are forms of welfare that people who work, and people who earn very high incomes, receive and people don't recognise that...

The need to break down this stigma around different welfare recipient "classes" is often cited as a precursor to being able to gain political support for UBI in the first place, but Camille (42 years) suggested that a UBI itself could also do this work if implemented:

> ...giving that money to everyone with no strings attached, no need to report in or ... do [what] they call mutual obligations, no need for any of that. If we just do it, people will accept it, because they'll see what good it does to the economy...

Camille (42 years) and Casey (47 years) both described their hope that a UBI might break down these false perceptions that people receiving social security are different or lesser than others, which is a primary cause of stigma. Casey (47 years) explained, "If everybody got UBI, I wonder whether … the feeling that somebody is getting an advantage [via social security receipt] would be taken away" (Casey, 47 years). As Emma (33 years) put it, "what's it going to mean for people's identities if they're not categorised [as social security recipients]? … I think people's lives would open up, their horizons would open up". Or as Casey (47 years) put it, UBI "could be the great equaliser".

As I explained in Chapter 3, the hypothetical UBI considered here would not replace social security payments altogether. Thus, whether this approach would entirely remove social-security-related stigma is questionable. As Casey (47 years) pointed out above, most of the population already receives "welfare" in one form or another, yet this is rarely made visible in stigmatising public discourses about welfare receipt. Nevertheless, as Korpi and Palme (1998, p. 36) convincingly argued in relation to what they call the "paradox of redistribution", "the more we target benefits at the poor only and the more concerned we are with creating equality via equal public transfers to all, the less likely we are to reduce poverty and inequality". A UBI would reduce the overall extent to which Australian cash transfers are targeted *only* to those living in poverty and would arguably be more visible than the subsidies and rebates described by Casey. This relates to Johnson et al.'s (2021, pp. 410–411) claim that

> One advantage of UBI schemes is that they mark out all members of society as equal in an important and visible sense: all get an equal share and do not have to go through assessments some find demeaning, in which they are powerless, in order to get it.

In this regard, a UBI would very likely *reduce* social-security-related stigmas, even if not removing them completely.

Conclusion

Ultimately, having a stable and guaranteed UBI can lead to significant behavioural changes, which can positively affect health over time (Johnson et al., 2022). This can mean shifting from short-term survival to longer-term planning. As Tam (55 years) explained:

> … When you don't have much money, you don't know what next month's going to bring. All you know is you're going to be living

> probably hand to mouth. But with knowing that money is coming in ... it helps you.

Tam likened a UBI to her experience over the past couple of years whereby, after spending years in survival mode on social security payments, she received an unexpected small inheritance payment, which she has put away as what she describes as a "contingency fund".

> It's been extraordinary for me over the last few years to have a contingency fund... To have that sitting there, and it's not a huge sum, but to have it in there is quite something... I realise I've [now] been thinking into the future and thinking long term instead of short-term survival mode. And you can plan.

For many women, this ability to think beyond immediate resource needs and plan for the future would also have significant impacts on reducing stress and improving mental health. By contrast, however, a UBI cannot (and arguably should not) ever be viewed as a simple "fix" for a problematic or failing public health system.

For many women, a UBI would certainly not replace systems and supports like Medicare, the PBS, and NDIS. However, as Bindi (31 years)—who is in the throes of trying to qualify for NDIS support—put it, with a UBI:

> I think I would [still apply for the NDIS support] but I wouldn't be so stressed about it because ... it wouldn't be like my survival is hinging on it because I cannot afford these things. I would just be like, "Okay, I'll just pay out of whatever money I have".

Ultimately, as the stories in this chapter again demonstrate, ensuring strong support for Australian women's health and well-being requires broader systemic changes that reduce health inequities overall. Greater attention to improving the universality of healthcare supports more broadly must be a crucial part of this future planning, even if alongside a UBI.

Notes

1 Australia's first national health insurance scheme, "Medibank", was originally introduced in 1975 under the Whitlam Government, though it was not until 1984 that it was reinstated under the new name "Medicare".

2 Of all private insurance general (ancillary) benefits paid to Australian policyholders in 2023–2024, 55% were for dental treatments, with the next highest category being optical treatments (16% of all benefits) (APRA, 2024).

6 Looking to the future

> It would give freedom from being afraid of the future... it [would] create better future generations... Taking care of women makes a much better society.
>
> (Eva, 58 years)

Across the stories recounted across this book so far, women express strong optimism about the potential benefits of UBI. This includes discussion of how a UBI might enhance economic security, reduce exposure to violence, improve health, and more. A core thread running through these stories is the overarching sense that UBI would ultimately improve women's freedom and ability to live more autonomously. As Bindi (31 years) explained, this can have ripple effects across all aspects of life:

> ...just having my own autonomy and agency over my life and being able to know that the choices I'm making [are] because I want to. It [UBI] just stops you from being taken advantage of by everyone. When I'm having to push aside my autonomy in one situation, like a work environment, that flows on into other environments too. I'm more likely to push aside my autonomy in friendships and in relationships and in just any other situation you can think of. Not being able to speak up and be authentic in one situation just erodes your authenticity in every other aspect.

Echoing Bindi's thoughts, Pateman (2004) proposes that UBI would ultimately provide a strong basis for expanding women's freedoms to be self-governing (see also Van Parijs, 1997). She explains, "Individual self-government depends not only on the opportunities available but also on the form of authority structure within which individuals interact with one another in their daily lives". UBI would influence these authority structures, freeing women (and indeed, all people) "not to be employed" nor depend on income from a partner or the state (Bueskens, 2017; Pateman, 2004, p. 92).

DOI: 10.4324/9781003586593-6

As Bindi pointed out, by removing the threat of destitution, UBI would mean women's life choices could better reflect their own needs and desires.

Women's stories also reinforce that context is important when considering UBI. Indeed, Australia's existing social security, tax, employment, and health policy landscape, as well as dominant social and gender norms, repeatedly inflected women's considerations about UBI's possible impacts. Relatedly, it is crucial to avoid framing UBI as a standalone solution for addressing gendered inequities (or indeed, any social issue). UBI alone will never be enough to eliminate the injustices faced by women; positioning it as such would set it up for inevitable failure. If, however, UBI is to *contribute* to improving women's overall position, it must be set at an adequate rate and paired with a suite of policy and program initiatives that uphold their basic rights and freedoms. Amongst other things, complementary initiatives must include genuine continued efforts to change dominant gender norms that subjugate women, including those that devalue care.

Ultimately, it is unclear whether a UBI is a realistic possibility for Australia's immediate future. Indeed, although women were overwhelmingly positive about its prospects, they—and many others in the broader UBI literature—caution that several barriers would first need to be overcome. One such barrier is the cost of implementing a UBI, which contributed to the perception amongst women interviewees that it remained a distant prospect:

> I guess one thought is just how would it really work? Because I think governments are struggling already at the moment to pay for things, pay for essential services, and we know they're in debt, because of all that spending that happened during the [COVID-19] pandemic...
>
> (Chandra, 33 years)

> I would think the government providing a decent amount of money to everybody is going to be pretty prohibitive regarding costs...
>
> (Erica, 65 years)

In a nationally representative survey I ran in November 2024 on the Australian public's attitudes towards UBI, respondents also ranked cost as one of their most significant concerns (Staines, 2025). Conversely, Tam (55 years) argued that even though cost matters, the future possibility of a UBI should not hinge on this consideration alone:

> So I just think it'd be hugely beneficial for society. I think we'd save heaps of money. But... I think society should measure itself by other things other than money, because why else do we exist? I think it'd [UBI] be really more humane.
>
> (Tam, 55 years)

Similarly to Tam, Pat (52 years) thought a UBI could produce:

> ... a positive [net] benefit, and it would save the government money from spending on a lot of [other services] ... basically I think prevention is better than cure in terms of anything to do with poverty—including health, prisons, so many problems that society has to spend money on—mopping up after the problem. If we started addressing it at the root cause we wouldn't need to spend this.

Indeed, these comments also point to the costs of *not* pursuing a UBI. Notwithstanding the importance of this, however, Jordan et al. (2021) have shown that framing UBI as too costly and unaffordable has a stronger impact on public opinion than other arguments, both for and against the policy. Thus, unless there is a palatable solution to the cost barrier for an Australian UBI, it is unlikely to receive broader support and traction.

Net outlays for several possible Australian UBIs, which involve diverse payment rates and tax reform options, range between $119.4 billion and $418.5 billion AUD per annum (Cowan, 2017; Phillips, 2018). Gross expenditure for the hypothetical UBI considered here would be substantial, though further modelling of net costs is required to also account for:

- efficiencies and savings from reduced use of other programs and services, including welfare, health, social services and more;
- lower poverty rates, resulting in lower associated expenditures to otherwise address the many lifelong social harms of poverty;
- the fact that UBI funds would be recouped from higher-income earners via the income tax system, thereby reducing the net cost; and
- possible tax reforms that could assist in funding a UBI, including the potential to increase taxes for the wealthiest Australians (Pereira, 2023).

Compared with other models proposed in Australia, the UBI rate considered here is also relatively generous (e.g., Ingles et al., 2019).

The international UBI literature identifies various funding avenues, ranging from progressive taxation reform (e.g., increases to income tax, wealth and/or inheritance taxes, increased corporate taxes), the integration of new taxes (e.g., robot and automation taxes), the use of resource or sovereign wealth funds, and more (Piketty, 2014; Standing, 2017; Ter-Minassian, 2020; Van Parijs & Vanderborght, 2017). In the Australian context, the detailed proposal for funding a Guaranteed Minimum Income (GMI) scheme presented by Henderson in the 1970s (discussed in Chapter 2), for instance, involved a linear tax rate of 40% on all private incomes (i.e., excluding GMI incomes) and a surtax on high incomes, which meant the GMI would be "self-financing" (Ingles et al., 2019; Saunders, 1981, p. 23). The political palatability of this approach today, however, is likely low. Indeed, The Greens' recently re-proposed wealth tax to fund cost-of-living-relief policies, including universal dentalcare, has been outright rejected by both major parties (Caporn et al., 2024; Jervis-Bardy, 2025). Meanwhile, Erica (65 years) also posited whether a sovereign wealth fund that accumulates capital from Australia's natural resources could be another possibility for financing a UBI, as occurs elsewhere in the world (e.g., Alaska Permanent Fund). In a settler colony like Australia, a wealth fund managed by the Australian Government off the back of the continent's natural resources raises significant ethical concerns. Indeed, it risks perpetuating settler colonial theft and extraction of lands and seas, upon which settler wealth has overwhelmingly been accumulated at the expense of First Nations peoples in the first place (Moreton-Robinson, 2015). It would also potentially frustrate efforts at advancing Treaty negotiations at both state and federal levels.

In the end, some have argued that it is impossible to design a UBI that would be large enough to achieve poverty reduction—including for women—while also being cost-effective and maintaining incentives to work (Cowan, 2017; Milligan, 2016). Conversely, others argue that a more realistic "stepping stone" approach to reform might involve gradually embedding characteristics of a UBI, such as unconditionality, into the existing social security and services system (Spies-Butcher & Henderson, 2019; Spies-Butcher et al., 2020). As Spies-Butcher et al. (2020, p. 517) explain, the model they propose:

> … takes current policy settings as a starting point, and moves towards universalism by individualising payments, removing non-income-based conditionality and reducing benefit withdrawal rates. While full implementation of these principles remains beyond short-term political possibilities, we argue that our findings reflect a surprising compatibility between Australia's existing benefit system and a modified BI that can inform debate over future efforts to reduce inequality and insecurity.

In another proposal, Bueskens (2017) advocates for a categorical basic income targeted at mothers. While supporting longer-term universality, she argues that targeting mothers is a natural first step that would "open up the possibility of a hitherto unseen equality that includes from dependence on a male wage". She argues that this is because such a policy would help overcome the so-called "motherhood penalty" of lost wages, career progression, lower superannuation, workplace discrimination and more that mothers tend to experience at higher rates—many of which were also referred to in women's accounts that featured in Chapter 3 (Lee & Craig, 2024). As also discussed in earlier chapters, however, this kind of "care income" has been shown to reinforce dominant gender norms around who undertakes care, rather than destabilising them (Cieplinski et al., 2023; also see Bibler et al., 2022). This is even more-so the case for an income designed to target *only* mothers, as per Bueskens' (2017) model, rather than *all* parents/primary caregivers notwithstanding gender. Moreover, it has a strong potential to undermine women's longer-term economic security, given a basic income would unlikely ever match the economic benefits of wage labour.

As an extension on Bueskens' (2017) proposal, another suggestion might be a UBI only for women. This was recommended, for example, by the United Nations Development Program (UNDP) as a temporary response to the COVID-19 pandemic, where they called for a temporary basic income (TBI) to support 613 million working-age women living in poverty worldwide (UNDP, 2021). To fund this measure, the UNDP (2021) called for governments across the globe to voluntarily redirect 0.07 of their respective GDPs towards a TBI fund. Returning to the Australian context, a UBI targeted at women and set at the right level could form part of a strategy to close Australia's gender pay gap overnight, dramatically increasing women's overall economic security. Again, however, this raises significant concerns. These include the potential for considerable political backlash in relation to the needs for equity and justice for low-income people of all genders, which would likely reduce broader support for UBI. Because of persistent targeting, such a scheme may also perpetuate the stigma associated with government support, while also doing little to address the core reasons for the pay gap in the first place. Indeed, a situation where women alone received an external financial supplement of this nature could actually worsen underlying gender pay gaps by reducing pressure on employers and policymakers to take other much-needed actions towards equity.

Quiggin et al.'s (2020a, 2020b) Liveable Income Guarantee (LIG) model represents another partial move towards UBI, acknowledging and celebrating non-waged work including caregiving, but without reinforcing gender norms. The LIG would operate like a "participation income", involving a payment at the age pension rate, which currently sits at 86% of the poverty line, to any Australian (16+ years of age) who does not have an "adequate market income [and] who is willing and able to contribute to Australian society" (Quiggin et al., 2020a, p. 5, 2020b). In this regard, it seeks to give "everyone the opportunity to contribute to society whether or not they generate a market income" and is designed to remunerate diverse forms of contribution, including "child-raising, study, volunteering, artistic and creative activity, community and ecological care" (Quiggin et al., 2020a, p. 3, 2020b). Notably, the proposed reporting mechanism is the self-assessment taxpayer declaration tool (via the Australian Taxation Office), which "remove[s] the presumption of cheating from those claiming benefits" (Quiggin et al., 2020a, p. 10, 2020b). Other supplementary payments, like Carer Payment, would continue alongside the LIG, with the overall cost being far more modest than full-blown UBI models. In 2020, this was estimated at $20 billion AUD per annum (Quiggin et al., 2020a, 2020b).

Ultimately, while these stepped approaches would likely achieve some of the positive outcomes that women pointed to in earlier chapters, they also hold risks. Indeed, if a UBI payment (or alternative cash transfer) is set too low, it is unlikely to be sufficient for adequately supporting caregivers and achieving the improvements in health, well-being, and freedom that women identified. If it is targeted only at women/mothers, there is a very real risk that it will limit their longer-term economic security and freedoms rather than enhancing them. If the approach involves removing conditionalities from existing social security payments, it would undoubtedly improve circumstances for many, but would still mean payment rates are unacceptably low while also doing little to address social security-related stigmas. It would also do little to tackle the effects of other gender-problematic social security policies identified in earlier chapters, such as the couple rule. Another important consideration for these kinds of stepped approaches is that, while they may partially address the cost barrier of implementing a UBI (or similar), they do not necessarily circumvent the strong commitment in the hearts and minds of most Australians to the centrality of a "paid work ethic". This creates a deep, ideological barrier to UBI, which must also be overcome if the policy is to gain traction.

As I canvassed in Chapter 2, the Australian tax and transfer system has long celebrated the significance and importance of paid work (Deeming, 2013), having been aptly characterised as a "wage-earner's welfare state" (Castles, 1985). This was powerfully articulated by former Australian Prime Minister Scott Morrison in his 2015 address to the National Press Club where he claimed: "...at the end of the day the best form of welfare is a job and creating jobs and getting people in a position to take one is even more important than systems reform itself" (Morrison, 2015, n.p.). This eulogization of paid work has underpinned decades of policymaking to erode social security safety nets. As previously discussed, this has included intensified conditionalities and refusals across the political spectrum to raise most social security payment rates above the poverty line, with the aim of ensuring paid work incentives remain intact (McKeever & Walsh, 2020). As women spoke about in Chapter 3, this has been incredibly harmful and spurred on by a divisive and stigmatising public discourse that positions social security recipients as "lazy" and irresponsible

(Marston et al. 2022; O'Connor, 2001; Saunders, 2019). For example, Jules (30 years) explained:

> So I think Australia would be, it [UBI] would be the right thing to do, but unfortunately I can't see it happening anytime soon, just based on how the government historically and currently have viewed the economy as something that essentially the poor have to fight their way through in order to have a liveable life, essentially... I think we let the very wealthy and wealthy corporations get away with not paying their fair share, and then we blame poor people for not trying hard enough to pull themselves out of poverty. But poverty isn't a personal failure...

Similar views were also reflected in the UBI survey I referred to earlier (Staines, 2025). There, respondents who did *not* support UBI tended to raise a perceived need to uphold the paid work ethic, as well as a strong sense of reciprocity, as key areas of concern. This included regular references to the apparent threat that UBI would disincentivise paid work, make people lazy, and act as an unreciprocated and potentially morally hazardous "handout" (McKeever & Walsh, 2020; O'Connor, 2001; Saunders, 2019). As one survey respondent put it, "I have been raised to believe money is earned, not handed to you for free". Such views tap into deeply held notions of fairness and justice, which in Australia continue to resonate with a meritocratic "fair go" and related "pull-yourself-up-by-the-bootstraps" approach to self-improvement (Crisp, 2022; Saunders, 2004). This is echoed in Elster's (1986, p. 719) argument *against* a UBI model proposed by van der Veen and van Parijs (1986), where he contends that it:

> ... goes against a widely accepted notion of justice: it is unfair for able-bodied people to live off the labour of others. Most workers would, correctly in my opinion, see the proposal as a recipe for exploitation of the industrious by the lazy.

Carroll and Engel (2021, p. 415) show that this anti-UBI sentiment appears frequently in Australian mainstream media, where the policy is regularly depicted as encouraging "idleness and laziness amongst the poor". For instance, one Australian Broadcasting Corporation (ABC) article in Carroll and Engel's (2021, p. 416) dataset explained "it is good for both the economy and the people in it to maintain a social stigma against long-term idleness". Of course, such arguments completely ignore the fact that many of those outside the labour force are far from idle, undertaking significant amounts of unpaid work, including extensive caregiving. Under such arrangements it is the *norm* for "able-bodied people to live off the labour of others"—or to be more precise, for whole economies and societies to function by 'free-riding' on women's unpaid labour (Elster 1986, p. 719; Fraser 2016; Holten 2025). These arguments about the paid work ethic also ignore strong evidence from UBI pilots across the globe that show overall labour force participation does *not* tend to reduce because of the policy. They also rarely consider the so-called "idle rich", who do not need to work, but instead live off passive income sources derived from inherited wealth, trust funds, and/or investments (stocks, property, etc.). Indeed, similar levels of public condemnation are rarely directed towards the wealthiest amongst us who are in this position. Nevertheless, it is no small task to challenge and/or reverse this ingrained thinking, which produces a "chicken and egg" scenario for the possibility of an Australian UBI. That is, even though UBI has been positioned as an important option for "respond[ing] to wedge politics that surrounds welfare debates" in Australia (Spies-Butcher, 2018, p. 1), broad public support would be needed to realistically pursue a UBI in the first place.

Shifting these entrenched attitudes is a major ongoing political challenge, but as Marston (2019, p. 38) acknowledges, it is also a "cultural challenge in terms of acknowledging the limits of the paid work ethic and accepting an alternative vision of human progress, based on non-material goods (such as wellbeing, discretionary time, and the right to realise our human capacities)". He goes on to add:

> A meta-framing of the policy problem [to which a UBI is responding] requires a radical departure from a dominant political and cultural discourse that accepts that the prosperity of a developed country can still be measured by continuous economic growth and jobs, irrespective of environmental and human costs.
>
> (Marston, 2019, p. 38)

Relatedly, and based on their 2019–2020 survey data on Australian public opinion around UBI, Patulny and Spies-Butcher (2023) argue that strategies for improving support must form consensus around both materialist and post-materialist arguments to address priorities across the political spectrum. This would include positioning UBI as a means of responding to increasing economic insecurity and inequality, as well as being capable of supporting post-materialist livelihoods (Patulny & Spies-Butcher, 2023). Similarly, in their future scenarios paper on UBI in Australia, Durnan and Inayatullah (2020, p. 102) argued:

> ...effective UBI introduction would require policy intervention to cast wider than welfare, education, tax and banking structure reform; policy levers would need to go further, to support the evolution of the Australian value set from foundational capitalist principles to social contribution and betterment.

This required "evolution" of Australian values would necessitate broad institutional support. Conversely, Australia's two major political parties remain largely hostile to UBI. As mentioned earlier, the country's media also tends to frame UBI in negative terms (Carroll & Engel, 2021), continuing to perpetuate stigmatising discourses around social security receipt that eulogise the primacy of paid work (Martin et al., 2022). Patulny and Spies-Butcher (2023) suggest a need for "long-term information campaigns on policy benefits of UBI" to counter these dominant discourses and widen overall support. This need to shift the values that underpin Australians' views on social support broadly is crucial to wider acceptance of UBI over time, as well as to the kinds of incremental moves that Spies-Butcher et al. (2020) and others have also discussed in relation to embedding UBI principles, like unconditionality, into Australia's existing social security system. The COVID-19 experience produced greater empathy for those without access to paid work, though this shift was temporary (Stambe & Marston, 2023). It remains to be seen whether more enduring crises, such as climate change, could have similar effects over the longer term.

Ultimately, the question of an Australian UBI is deeply complex. This complexity arises not only from the need to determine an appropriate payment amount and funding source, but also from the challenge of designing a policy that maximises positive impacts, dispels fears around idleness, and can secure broad public support. Additionally, any UBI proposal must also consider necessary tax reforms and adjustments to existing social security and related programs to balance competing priorities. None of this is easy or straightforward, and I do not claim to provide definitive answers on the future of an Australian UBI here. However, what I hope this book *does* reinforce is that any future deliberations on UBI or alternative policies should be assessed through an intersectional gender lens to make visible their relative impacts for women, but also those living at the multiple intersections of race, ability, age, class, and more. This is crucial for ensuring that future policymaking contributes to tackling and reducing existing social inequalities, rather than exacerbating them. In the meantime, the accounts that women so generously shared in previous chapters also point to other immediate policy reforms, which might have significant impacts regardless of whether a UBI is ultimately introduced. I touch on some of these below.

Getting the wider policy and program architecture right for Australian women

The reform suggestions that follow are in no way intended as a comprehensive list of actions arising from the women's stories shared in this book. Rather, they are starting points, aimed at addressing at least *some* of the issues that women repeatedly raised. What are missing from this below list, for example, are desperately needed major reforms to Australia's housing market, which sees so many people locked out of secure, safe, and affordable housing. Crucially, part of the solution must be increased investment in social housing—particularly public housing—where Australia continues to fall woefully behind other OECD nations (AHURI, 2022). Another key piece of the puzzle is improving Australia's healthcare system, to promote universal access to quality care. This must involve ongoing reforms to the interlocking elements of this broad system, including Medicare, the NDIS, and PBS. As part of this, continued attention to the availability and affordability of mental health services is also desperately needed, including to ensure that all individuals can access appropriate, safe, and timely diagnoses and support. Finally, Australians must continue to address hegemonic gender norms that continue to subjugate women. Ongoing efforts to challenge these norms are essential to achieving gender equity, ensuring that women have equal access to power, resources, and recognition. In addition to these much-needed structural changes, this research also points to more specific incremental reforms. While I have already touched on some of these in earlier chapters, I outline them again briefly below.

Reassessing Australia's couple rule

One characteristic of UBI that resonated strongly with women was that it is an individual payment (BIEN, 2023) and not contingent on the receipt of other individual or household income/s. As described in earlier chapters, and elsewhere (e.g., Griffiths, 2017; Sleep, 2019, 2023), Australia's "couple rule" runs contrary to this, positioning couples as a single financial unit for the purpose of allocating means-tested social security benefits and subsidies (e.g., Childcare Subsidy). There are limited and very specific occasions where couples might be exempt from this treatment, such as where pooling resources is not an option due to one member being "required to move interstate… to attend legal proceedings", "living overseas awaiting residency application", being "subject to a newly arrived residents waiting period and unable to work", or "due to court ordered conditions … in rehabilitation or subject to parole resulting in separate living arrangements" (Australian Government, 2025). Outside of these specific instances, an exemption is unlikely. Notably, for instance, exemptions are not offered where "a couple is able to pool resources but *chooses* not to do so" (my emphasis added, Australian Government, 2025).

Other research has found that the couple rule disproportionately disadvantages women, meaning their relationship statuses are subject to continual policing by the state (Sleep, 2019, 2023; Yamamori, 2014).

In practice, the rule increases the effective marginal tax rate for the lower income earning person in a couple, who is typically female in heterosexual couples, and thereby renders them at least to some extent dependent on their spouse (Sleep, 2019, 2023; Griffiths, 2017). Additionally, Australia's joint social security payments, like Family Tax Benefits, are paid into one person's bank account and cannot be split between multiple accounts to be shared equally by multiple individuals. This can also disadvantage women, especially in relationships where abuse is present and where hoarding of resources by one partner is used to establish or maintain power over the other, as was the case in multiple women's stories here.

A simple, albeit expensive, reform option would be to abolish the couple rule and treat individuals separately (Griffiths, 2017). Alternatively, Griffiths (2017) suggests that other more incremental reforms may include:

- establishing a "grace period" for new couples, within which they continue to be treated independently despite cohabiting,
- introducing a "top-up"/additional work allowance for household second earners, and/or
- enabling couples to arrange for joint payments to be split across two independently managed accounts.

As described earlier, a UBI would at least partly overcome this problem by enabling independent access to an individual unconditional income for all—even though this does not prevent partners from gaining access to/control over a partner's UBI. In the meantime, however, reassessing the impact and cost of amending the couple rule in Australia should be a priority, with a view to supporting women's access to independent incomes.

Improving access to escaping violence payments

An independent income for women was also viewed by interviewees in this study as crucial for enabling them to escape violence. Aside, however, from Australia's highly conditional and gendered social security system, and ad hoc support available from the charitable sector (which varies in availability and quality), Australian women have few places to turn for economic support to leave violent relationships. In an effort to remedy this, in October 2021, the Australian Government established a two-year pilot "Escaping Violence Payment" (EVP), which is administered by third-sector provider UnitingCare and provides emergency access to up to $5,000 in funding (i.e., up to $1,500 cash and $3,500 in non-cash goods, services, and support) to victims of domestic and family violence in order to "reduce… financial barriers associated with leaving" (DSS, 2023b, p. 3). As I explained in Chapter 4, 89% of those accessing the program are women (DSS, 2023b), though access can be complicated by several barriers.

Between July and September 2023, more than half of those applying for the EVP were rejected, having been deemed ineligible for myriad reasons, including not having the right documentation such as doctor's reports, or being unable to demonstrate financial hardship as they did not have a bank account in their name (Kelly, 2024). This indicates core problems with the program design, which fundamentally mistrusts those who seek these payments (primarily women), placing the onus on them to turn to others, such as medical professionals, to substantiate their claims of victimisation *before* they can access financial support. This approach also fails to acknowledge that not having a bank account in one's own name can be a *symptom* of both abuse *and* financial hardship. Turning women away on this basis is alarming, to say the least.

In a country where access to medical services can be incredibly costly, and where domestic, family, and sexual violence also remains rife, it seems obvious that EVPs should at the very least be provided in an immediate and urgent manner, enabling the claims of those seeking support to be taken as *prima facie* truth. If accountability checks are to be undertaken, these should be post hoc to avoid victims being unable to access payments at the time they are most needed. Ultimately, this again draws attention to the administrative simplicity of a UBI, whereby women would not be at risk of being deemed ineligible for independent financial support.

Improving access to commodified care options

As discussed in Chapter 3, another key factor for improving women's long-term economic security and freedom is better access to high-quality and affordable commodified care, including aged care and childcare. This has been a longstanding policy challenge in Australia, where there is an ongoing shortage of childcare centres and services, and where those that do exist are either extremely expensive or have increasingly long wait-lists—often both (Brennan, 1998; Coorey, 2024; Fuller, 2024; Gould, 2025). Hurley et al. (2022) reported that centre-based day care services for children aged zero to four years are difficult to access overall, but especially so in regional and remote areas and for those on low incomes. Their 2022 study reports that approximately ~35.2% of the total Australian population lives in "childcare deserts"—"areas where childcare is most scarce", defined as having fewer than 0.333 childcare places per child in the local population (Hurley et al., 2022, p. 4). For First Nations families, as well as those from other culturally and linguistically diverse backgrounds, an additional challenge is finding childcare that is culturally appropriate and safe (Hurley et al., 2022; Klein et al., 2024).

Australia's early childhood care system continues to undergo reform, including in response to a recent Productivity Commission (2024) inquiry, which recommended steps towards universal access. Recently, the Australian Government passed legislation to remove the Childcare Subsidy activity test—which linked eligibility to a recipient's work, training, study, or volunteering hours—and instead guarantees a minimum of three days of subsidised childcare for all Australian families, with a slightly higher allowance for First Nations families (Clare & Aly, 2025). The new subsidy will take effect from January 2026. However, it remains unclear whether further steps will be taken towards a fully universal system, as recommended by the Productivity Commission (2024).

Notwithstanding its importance in the overall policy landscape, commodified care cannot be the only response to improving women's economic security and freedoms. Indeed, we also need policies that do not simply reinforce the universal breadwinner model, but which also recognise and adequately support the value of caregiving in all forms. This re-emphasises the potential of UBI to open opportunities for better centring care, including through support for a universal caregiver model that celebrates rather than sidelines this most crucial social contribution.

Amending existing Australian social security

Other characteristics of UBI that resonated most in the interviews were its *unconditionality* (BIEN, 2023) and—in relation to the scenario of a UBI paid at the Henderson Poverty Line—its *adequacy* when compared with most of Australia's existing social security payments. For many of the women who were themselves either current or past social security recipients, these were both incredibly important design features for the Australian context. In lieu of a full UBI for Australia, and as discussed earlier, others have suggested the possibility of taking incremental steps towards a UBI by "turning off" non-means-testing-related conditionalities within Australian social security and improving the adequacy of social security payments (Ingles et al., 2019; Spies-Butcher et al., 2023). This would essentially mimic a categorical UBI, maintaining a level of fiscal efficiency through means-testing and targeting.

As Klein et al. (2022a, 2022b) point out, social policy changes during the COVID-19 pandemic in Australia mimicked an emergency, categorical basic income, providing important insight into what might be expected from this approach in future. During this time, for instance, a Coronavirus Supplement Payment meant that the JobSeeker unemployment benefit essentially doubled from 27 April 2020, before being tapered off towards the end of that year and returning to base rates on 31 March 2021 (Staines & Zahnow, 2022). This temporarily lifted benefit recipients above the Henderson Poverty Line. In addition, and due to COVID-19 lockdown orders, mutual obligations were also suspended. Thus, for a short period, this rendered a raft of social security payments effectively unconditional, although eligibility means-testing/targeting did still apply.

The impacts of these changes were profound, with studies finding that social security recipients were more able to meet their basic needs, experienced improved physical and emotional health and well-being, increased their labour-market engagement, and were also more able to engage in other forms of important productive work, including caregiving (Klein et al., 2021). Higher incomes also improved the affordability of healthy foods (Lewis & Lee, 2020), reduced housing stress (Phillips et al., 2020; Raynor & Panza, 2021), and significantly lowered general financial stress, which produced general improvements in mental health (Botha et al., 2022). Overall, the changes resulted in a 17-year low poverty rate after nearly 20 years of little movement at all (ACOSS, 2022). This drastically, though temporarily, improved the lives of thousands of the most marginalised Australians, including thousands of women, their dependents, and communities (Klein et al., 2021). Though, as Botha et al. (2022) suggest, these findings were fleeting; permanent measures may produce more lasting effects.

As described earlier, Australians' strong ideological commitment to the paid work ethic presents a continued challenge to proposals for raising social security payment rates and removing activity-related conditions. Notwithstanding this, there remain current proposals from Australia's minor parties, such as The Greens, to pursue a similar model, which would see a return to a Commonwealth Employment Service (CES) (rather than Australia's quasi-marketized employment services sector) and the removal of mutual obligations (The Greens, 2025). If the recent 2025 federal election result—where The Greens lost nearly all seats in the House of Representatives—is taken as even a partial indication of this proposal's popularity, then there is some way to go before it is realised in reality (Bachelard & Lucas, 2025).

While this strategy holds many potential long-term benefits, it does not address what Korpi and Palme (1998) refer to as the "redistribution paradox". That is, the idea that targeting social assistance weakens public and political support for social security because not everyone is included as a recipient. Thus, while a stepping-stone approach could significantly improve recipients' material conditions and reduce the harms associated with mutual obligations, it is unlikely to reduce stigma in the way that a UBI might.

(Re)prioritising collective bargaining

As discussed in Chapter 3, women highlighted that a UBI could provide the economic security needed to strengthen their choices and bargaining power in paid work. This relates to broader changes in Australian industrial relations policies, which have weakened unions and prioritised individual over collective bargaining, disproportionately affecting low-paid women (Pocock et al., 2008; Stanford et al., 2022). This erosion of collective bargaining in Australia has been described as the "fourth worst of any OECD country" (Stanford et al., 2022, p. 4). Women are particularly at risk from such changes because they tend to fare worse than men in bargaining negotiations, further reinforcing the gender pay gap (Recalde & Vesterlund, 2023; WGEA, 2018). However, union membership mitigates this disadvantage, with unionised women earning nearly 30% more per week than non-unionised women—an advantage that exceeds the 25% "union advantage" observed amongst men (Pennington & Stanford, 2020, p. 57).

Policy responses that take a "fix the women" approach by encouraging women to negotiate more like men yield limited success (Recalde & Vesterlund, 2023). Instead, greater emphasis should be placed on addressing structural factors that contribute to these outcomes. As previously discussed, a UBI could provide individuals with a small but stable source of income, potentially enhancing their bargaining power. However, additional measures, such as reprioritising collective over individual bargaining, are also necessary as part of a broader policy framework to support women's long-term economic security (Lazar, 2020; Recalde & Vesterland, 2023; Stanford et al., 2022).

Concluding remarks

The strategies outlined above are far from exhaustive, though they do suggest some starting points for reform to address the main challenges that women discussed in earlier chapters. Notwithstanding these, and despite persistent barriers, the potential benefits of a UBI for Australian women are also clear. This simple but powerful policy approach holds strong potential for improving several outcomes for women. At the same time, UBI is not a cure-all and must be considered alongside other policy architectures that are also gender sensitive, as well as broader efforts to destabilise harmful hegemonic gender norms.

Exactly 50 years ago, former Prime Minister Gough Whitlam identified these same social norms as a key reason for the many injustices Australian women faced. He explained:

> The cause lies invariably in the deeply ingrained cultural assumptions that every woman's primary role is that of daughter, wife, mother, mother-in-law, or grandmother; nurse, secretary, teacher, or shop assistant; the deeply ingrained assumption that women are here to serve or assist.
>
> (Whitlam in Reid, 2023, p. 15)

In many ways and against many metrics, outcomes for women have improved, though this remains uneven across the added intersections of race, class, ability, and more. In other ways, outcomes for women have worsened, particularly regarding access to state supports that are non-punitive and non-stigmatising. What remains consistent is that the same gendered social norms that so deeply inflected women's livelihoods and outcomes during Whitlam's prime ministership are still alarmingly present today. This came through repeatedly in the stories that women shared in this book, from those about juggling their many caregiving responsibilities to the ways that they felt unsupported by myriad state-provided services that were ostensibly designed to *help* them, but that were often experienced as unhelpful or, at worst, harmful. It also came through strongly in their many stories of violence victimisation and discrimination. Ultimately, as I mentioned at the outset of this book, these women's stories indicate incredible resilience and strength, but also deep frustrations with the economic insecurities thrust upon them by systems and policies that are not designed *by* or *for* them. If the women interviewed in this book were in charge of designing these systems for themselves—to truly support their needs and address their challenges—they would look very different.

Ultimately, irrespective of whether a UBI is ever implemented in Australia, urgent reform is needed to support women's economic security, autonomy, and "real freedoms" now and in the future. As Casey (47 years) provocatively asked at the start of this book, "if women had that bit more of control or autonomy over their own lives, perhaps the world wouldn't get away with the way that it treats women". It is my hope that this book might contribute, even in some small way, to ongoing discussions not only about UBI but also the broader policy changes needed to improve outcomes for women across Australia and beyond. Ultimately, a just future is one where a person's economic security, safety, health, and freedom are not determined by the sex they are assigned at birth, nor the gender they choose to move through life with. Although that future remains within our reach, there is still a great deal of work to do.

To end this book as I began, I will leave the final word to one of the interviewees themselves. Whatever approach we take to imagining and pursuing the "good life" in Australia and beyond, it needs to be one that "would allow a lot more people to live with dignity in a way that they choose… [and] enable more people to thrive instead of just surviving" (Marley, 35 years).

Bibliography

ABS. (2001). *Australian social trends, 2001 – Health expenditure: private health insurance.* https://www.abs.gov.au/ausstats/abs@.nsf/2f762f95845417aeca25706c00834efa/0aaf3311ebcd3646ca2570ec000c46e4!OpenDocument

ABS. (2021a). *Australia – 2021 Census all persons QuickStats.* Retrieved November 11, 2024, from https://www.abs.gov.au/census/find-census-data/quickstats/2021/AUS

ABS. (2021b). *Australia – Aboriginal and/or Torres Strait Islander peoples profile.* Retrieved January 7, 2025, from https://abs.gov.au/census/find-census-data/community-profiles/2021/AUS/download/IP_AUS.xlsx

ABS. (2022). *ABS statement on 2021 Census non-binary sex count.* Retrieved November 11, 2024, from https://www.abs.gov.au/media-centre/media-statements/abs-statement-2021-census-non-binary-sex-count#:~:text=The%20Australian%20Bureau%20of%20Statistics,Male'%20and%20'Female

ABS. (2023). *Earnings and working conditions – average weekly earnings Australia, May 2023.* https://www.abs.gov.au/statistics/labour/earnings-and-working-conditions/average-weekly-earnings-australia/may-2023

ABS. (2024b). *Disability, ageing and carers, Australia: summary of findings.* https://www.abs.gov.au/statistics/health/disability/disability-ageing-and-carers-australia-summary-findings/latest-release#:~:text=In%202022%2C%205.5%20million%20(21.4,million%20(17.7%25)%20in%202018

ABS. (2025b). *Labour force, Australia – January 2025.* Retrieved February 27, 2025, from. https://www.abs.gov.au/statistics/labour/employment-and-unemployment/labour-force-australia/jan-2025#:~:text=In%20trend%20terms%2C%20in%20January,employment%20increased%20to%2014%2C616%2C400

ACOSS. (2021). *How social security works against women: overview of key issues facing women receiving income support.* ACOSS & National Council of Single Mothers and their Children. https://www.acoss.org.au/wp-content/uploads/2021/09/210906-Social-security-and-how-it-works-against-women-final.pdf

ACOSS. (2022). *Poverty in Australia 2022: a snapshot.* ACOSS. https://povertyandinequality.acoss.org.au/wp-content/uploads/2022/10/Poverty-in-Australia-2020_A-snapshot.pdf

ACOSS. (2024b, May 6). *Women leaders call for JobSeeker boost to promote women's safety.* https://www.acoss.org.au/media_release/women-leaders-call-for-jobseeker-boost-to-promote-womens-safety/

Australian Government Commission of Inquiry into Poverty ('Henderson Inquiry'). (1975). *First main report.* https://nla.gov.au/nla.obj-1357060179

Australian Human Rights Commission. (2025). *National children's commissioner calls for urgent action to safeguard children in early learning and care.* https://humanrights.gov.au/about/news/media-releases/national-childrens-commissioner-calls-urgent-action-safeguard-children

AHURI. (2022). *What is the right level of social housing for Australia?* https://www.ahuri.edu.au/analysis/brief/what-right-level-social-housing-australia

AIHW. (2019). *People with disability in Australia.* AIHW. https://www.aihw.gov.au/reports/disability/people-with-disability-in-australia-in-brief/contents/how-many-people-have-disability

AIHW. (2024a). *Health and wellbeing of First Nations people.* https://www.aihw.gov.au/reports/australias-health/indigenous-health-and-wellbeing

AIHW. (2024b). *Mental health.* https://www.aihw.gov.au/mental-health/overview/prevalence-and-impact-of-mental-illness

AIHW. (2024c). *People with disability in Australia.* Available: https://www.aihw.gov.au/reports/disability/people-with-disability-in-australia/contents/summary

Alburez-Gutierrez, D., Mason, C. & Zagheni, E. (2021). The 'sandwich generation' revisited: global demographic drivers of care time demands. *Population and Development Review, 47*(4), 997–1023.

Ali Hussen, D. (2023, June 4). Universal basic income of £1,600 a month to be trialled in two places in England. *The Guardian.* https://www.theguardian.com/society/2023/jun/04/universal-basic-income-of-1600-pounds-a-month-to-be-trialled-in-england

Alstott, A. (2001). Good for women. In V. Parijs (Ed.), *What's wrong with a free lunch?* chapter 27. Beacon Press.

Altman, J., & Markham, F. (2019). Basic income and cultural participation for remote-living Indigenous Australians. In. E. Klein, J. Mays, & T. Dunlop (Eds.), *Implementing a basic income in Australia: Pathways forward* (pp. 87–109).

Amnesty International. (2016). *Australia: appalling abuse, neglect of refugees on Nauru.* https://www.health.gov.au/ministers/the-hon-mark-butler-mp/media/private-health-insurance-premiums-rise-less-than-wages-pensions-and-inflation

Angeles, M. R., Crosland, P., & Hensher, M. (2023). Challenges for Medicare and universal health care in Australia since 2000. *Medical Journal of Australia, 218*(7), 285–331.

Anglicare Australia. (2021). *Valuing every contribution: What basic income would mean for Australians.* https://www.anglicare.asn.au/wp content/uploads/2021/08/Australia-Fair-Valuing-Every-Contribution.pdf

Anishinaabe, E. J., Doucet, A., Falk, J., & Mohawk, K. H. (2022). 'Looking after our own is what we do': Urban Ontario indigenous perspectives on juggling paid work and unpaid care work for adult family members. *Wellbeing, Space and Society, 3*(100102), 1–10.

Anthony, T. (2017, June 6). *Factcheck: Are First Australians the most imprisoned people on earth?* The Conversation. https://theconversation.com/factcheck-are-first-australians-the-most-imprisoned-people-on-earth-78528

Arrow, M. (Ed.) (2023). *Women and Whitlam: Revisiting the revolution.* NewSouth Publishing.

Arthur, D. (2016). *Basic income: A radical idea enters the mainstream.* Parliamentary Library, Parliament of Australia.

Australian Broadcasting Corporation (ABC) News. (2024, May 7). *Students expelled from Yarra Valley Grammar over spreadsheet that used offensive terms to describe female pupils.* https://www.abc.net.au/news/2024-05-07/boys-expelled-from-yarra-valley-grammar/103813488

Australian Bureau of Statistics (ABS). (2024a, August). *Characteristics of employment, Australia.* https://www.abs.gov.au/statistics/labour/earnings-and-working-conditions/characteristics-employment-australia/aug-2024

Australian Bureau of Statistics (ABS). (2024c). *Life expectancy.* https://www.abs.gov.au/statistics/people/population/life-expectancy/latest-release

Australian Bureau of Statistics (ABS). (2025a). *Population clock and pyramid.* Retrieved February 27, 2025, from https://www.abs.gov.au/statistics/people/population/population-clock-pyramid

Australian Council of Social Services (ACOSS). (2024a). *About the campaign.* Raise the Rate for Good. https://www.raisetherate.org.au/about_the_campaign

Australian Government. (n.d.). *Multicultural Australia – united, strong, successful: Australia's multicultural statement.* Australian Government, Department of Home Affairs. https://www.homeaffairs.gov.au/mca/Statements/english-multicultural-statement.pdf

Australian Government. (2024). *2024 status of women report card.* Australian Government. https://genderequality.gov.au/status-women-report-cards/2024-report-card

Australian Government. (2025). *Guides to social policy law, Family Assistance Guide – Version 1.261, released 2 January 2025.* https://guides.dss.gov.au/family-assistance-guide/3/5/2/10#:~:text=CA%20recipients%20who%20report%20more,3%20of%20the%20activity%20test)

Australian Housing and Urban Research Institute (AHURI). (2021). *What the 2021 Census data told us about homelessness.* https://www.ahuri.edu.au/analysis/brief/what-2021-census-data-told-us-about-homelessness#:~:text=Whereas%20the%202016%20census%20saw,of%20every%2010%2C000%20in%202021

Australian Human Rights Commission (AHRC). (2019). *Older women's risk of homelessness: Background paper.*

Australian Institute of Health and Welfare (AIHW). (2023a). *Family, domestic and sexual violence: Economic and financial impacts.* https://www.aihw.gov.au/family-domestic-and-sexual-violence/responses-and-outcomes/economic-financial-impacts

Australian Institute of Health and Welfare (AIHW). (2023b). *The health of Australia's females.* https://www.aihw.gov.au/reports/men-women/female-health/contents/how-healthy

Australian Prudential Regulatory Authority (APRA). (2024, December). *Annual private health insurance statistics.* https://www.apra.gov.au/sites/default/files/2024-12/20241213%20-%20Annual%20private%20health%20insurance%20membership%20and%20benefits%20statistics.xlsx

Australian Psychological Society (APS). (2025). *How much does seeing a psychologist cost?* https://psychology.org.au/psychology/about-psychology/what-it-costs

Australian Tax Office (ATO). (2024). *Individual statistics – Individuals summary tables and charts.* https://www.ato.gov.au/about-ato/research-and-statistics/in-detail/taxation-statistics/taxation-statistics-2021-22/statistics/individuals-statistics#Table3Individuals

Azize, M. (2021). *Valuing every contribution: what a basic income would mean for Australians.* https://www.anglicare.asn.au/wp-content/uploads/2021/08/Australia-Fair-Valuing-Every-Contribution.pdf

Azize, M. (2023). *Brutal reality: The human cost of Australia's housing crisis.* Everybody's Home. https://fha.org.au/wp-content/uploads/2023/07/EH_Brutal-Reality-Report_2023.pdf

Bacchi, C. (2009). *Analysing policy: What's the problem represented to be?* Pearson.

Bachelard, M. & Lucas, C. (2025). Greens leave: after 15 years, how Bandt and his party won, and lost, in Melbourne. *The Age.* https://www.theage.com.au/politics/victoria/greens-leave-after-15-years-how-bandt-and-his-party-won-and-lost-in-melbourne-20250508-p5lxqz.html

Barrett, J. (2017). Why the Australasian tradition of labour defence is a barrier to a universal basic income. *Journal of Australian Taxation, 19*(2), 1–24.

Basic Income Earth Network (BIEN). (2023). *Home: What is basic income?* https://basicincome.org/

Beaufils, J. (2023). 'That's the bloodline': Does kinship and care translate to kinship care? *Australian Journal of Social Issues, 58*(2), 296–317.

Bessant, J., & Watts, R. (2021). Covid, capital and the future of work in Australia. *Australian Quarterly, 92*(1), 20–28.

Bueskens, P. (2019). 'Gillard's dilemma, *The Sexual Contract* and maternal citizenship: the case of Australian single mothers', In. Pascoe Leahy, C., & Bueskens, P. (Eds.) *Australian mothering: historical and sociological perspectives*, pp. 421–435. Palgrave Macmillan.

Bibler, A., Guettabi, M. & Reiner, M. (2023). Universal cash transfers and labour market outcomes. *Journal of Policy Analysis and Management, 42*(1), 198–224.

Bick, A., & Fuchs-Schündeln, N. (2017). Quantifying the disincentive effects of joint taxation on married women's labor supply. *American Economic Review, 107*(5), 100–104.

Bidadanure, J. U. (2019). The political theory of universal basic income. *Annual Review of Political Science, 22*, 481–501.

Biddle, N., Edwards, B., Gray, M., & McEachern, S. (2022). *Is the universal basic income for us?* https://whataustraliathinks.org.au/data_story/is-the-universal-basic-income-for-us/

Blaxland, M. (2010). Mothers and mutual obligation. In Goodwin, S., & Huppatz, K. (Eds.), *The good mother*, pp. 131–152. Sydney University Press.

Blofield, M., Cuartas, J., Filgueira, F., Franzoni, J. M., & Sánchez-Ancochea, D. (2022). *Towards a global universal basic income for children.* Think7 Policy Brief. https://social.desa.un.org/sites/default/files/inline-files/2022%20Toward-a-global-universal-basic-income-for-children%20Blofield_Cuartas_Filgueira_Martinez-Franzoni_Sanchez-Ancochea.pdf

Botha, F., Butterworth, P., & Wilkins, R. (2022). Protecting mental health during periods of financial stress: Evidence from the Australian Coronavirus Supplement income support payment. *Social Science & Medicine, 306*(115158), 1–7.

Branley, A., & Thorne, L. (2024, February 25). *Falling bulk-billing rates hit working families who don't qualify for concession cards.* ABC News. https://www.abc.net.au/news/2024-02-25/data-shows-gp-doctor-bulk-billing-rates-for-adult-patients/103505690

Braun, V., & Clarke, V. (2021). *Thematic analysis: A practical guide.* Sage.

Brennan, D. (2019). The good mother in Australian childcare policy, In Pascoe Leahy, C., & Bueskens, P. (Eds.) *Australian mothering: Historical and sociological perspectives*, pp. 339–358. Palgrave Macmillan.

Brennan, D. (1998). *The politics of Australian childcare: Philanthropy to feminism and beyond*. Cambridge University Press.

Briggs, C., & Buchanan, J. (2000). *Australian labour market deregulation: A critical assessment*. Australian Parliament. https://parlinfo.aph.gov.au/parlInfo/search/display/display.w3p;query=(Id:library/prspub/u1p16);rec=0;#:~:text=The%20first%20phase%20of%20labour%20deregulation%20occurred%20between%201987%20and,the%20future%20of%20wage%20fixing

Brotherhood of St Laurence. (2017). *Basic income: Trade-offs and Bottom lines*. Brotherhood of St Laurence.

Bryson, L. (1992). *Welfare and the state*. Bloomsberg.

Bueskens, P. (2017). Poverty-traps and pay-gaps: Why (single) mothers need basic income. In T. Hollo (Ed.), *Views of a universal basic income: Perspectives from across Australia*. The Green Institute.

Butler, M. (2024, March 5). *Private health insurance premiums rise less than wages, pensions and inflation*. Press Release by The Hon Mark Butler MP. https://www.amnesty.org/en/latest/press-release/2016/08/australia-abuse-neglect-of-refugees-on-nauru/

Cameron, A., & Tedds, L. (2021). *Gender-based violence, economic security, and the potential of basic income: A discussion paper*. University of Calgary & Women's Shelters Canada.

Cammett, A. (2014). Deadbeat dads and welfare queens: How metaphor shapes poverty law. *Boston College Journal of Law and Social Justice*, *34*(2), 233–265.

Campbell, I., & Burgess, J. (2018). Patchy progress? Two decades of research on precariousness and precarious work in Australia. *Labour and Industry*, *28*(1), 48–67.

Caporn, D., Jervis-Bardy, D., & Ransley, E. (2024, August 28). Adam Bandt's 'Robin Hood' tax reforms blasted as 'economic sabotage' from the greens. *The Nightly*.

Carey, G., Malbon, E., & Blackwell, J. (2021). Administering inequality? The National Disability Insurance Scheme and administrative burdens on individuals. *Australian Journal of Public Administration*, *80*(4), 854–872.

Care for Kids. (2025). *Costs of childcare – calculator*. https://www.careforkids.com.au/home/childcarecosts

Carroll, L., & Engel, S. (2021). Framing basic income in Australia: How the media is shaping the debate. *Australian Journal of Political Science*, *56*(4), 410–427.

Cassiman, S. (2008). Of witches, welfare queens, and the disaster named poverty: the search for a counter-narrative. *Journal of Poverty*, *10*(4), 51–66.

Castañeda, C. J. (2023). *Delayed and denied: a phenomenological investigation of women with autism and their experiences with late diagnosis* [PhD dissertation]. Texas Technical University.

Castles, F. (1985). *Working class and welfare: Reflections on the political development of the welfare state in Australia and New Zealand, 1890-1980*. Allen & Unwin Port Nicholson Press.

Cavadino & Dignan. (2006). Penal policy and political economy. *Criminology & Criminal Justice*, *6*(4), 435–456.

Chalmers, J. (2022, March 8). *Address to the Future Women Leadership Summit.* https://jimchalmers.org/latest-news/speeches/address-to-the-future-women-leadership-summit/

Champoux-Paillé, L., & Croteau, A. M. (2023, July 27). *The progress of women in the workplace is at a standstill. How can we break through the glass ceiling?* The Conversation. https://theconversation.com/the-progress-of-women-in-the-workplace-is-at-a-standstill-how-can-we-break-through-the-glass-ceiling-210247

Chiappero-Martinetti, E. (2014). Basic needs. In A. Michalos (Ed.), *Encyclopedia of quality of life and wellbeing research.* Springer Nature.

Chingaipe, S. (2024). *Black convicts: How slavery shaped Australia.* Simon & Schuster.

Chrisp, J. (2023, July 5). Relative poverty and UBI: unhappy bedfellows [Presentation]. *Social Policy Association (UK) Conference.* University of Nottingham, England.

Chung, M. (Ed.) (2023). *Basic income in Korea and beyond: Social, economic, and theological perspectives.* Palgrave Macmillan.

Cieplinski, A., D'Alessandro, S., Dwarkasing, C., & Guarnieri, P. (2023). Narrowing women's time and income gaps: An assessment of the synergies between working time reduction And universal income schemes. *World Development*, *167*, 1–25.

Clare, J., & Aly, A. (2025). *Albanese Government passes legislation to deliver child care three day guarantee.* Joint Media Release. https://ministers.education.gov.au/clare/albanese-government-introduces-legislation-guarantee-3-days-early-education-and-care

Clarke, A. (2023). Can a basic income help address homelessness? A Titmussian perspective. *Journal of Sociology*, *59*(4), 860–878.

Clarke, P., & Cutler, H. (2024). A proposal to extend universal insurance to dental care in Australia. *The Australian Economic Review*, *57*(2), 168–173.

Clarkson, C., Jacobs, Z., Marwick, B., Fullagar, R., Wallis, L., Smith, M., Roberts, R., Hayes, E., Lowe, K., Carah, X., Florin, A., McNeil, J., Cox, D., Arnold, L., Hua, Q., Huntley, J., Brand, H., Manne, T., Fairbairn, A. [...] & Pardoe, C. (2017). Human occupation of northern Australia by 65,000 years ago. *Nature*, *547*, 306–326.

Coleman, M. (2023). Women's health, women's welfare, In. Arrow, M. (Ed.) *Women and Whitlam: revisiting the revolution*, pp. 119–138. NewSouth Publishing.

Collie, A., Sheehan, L. & Jane, T. (2021). Changes in access to Australian disability support benefits during a period of social welfare reform. *Journal of Social Policy*, *51*(1), 132–154.

Conner, D. H. (2014). Financial freedom: Women, money, and domestic abuse. *William & Mary Journal of Women and the Law*, *20*(2), 339–398.

Cook, K. (2019). Gender, social security, and poverty. In P. Saunders (Ed.), *Revisiting Henderson: Poverty, social security, and basic income*, chapter 12. Melbourne University Publishing.

Coorey, P. (2024, August 8). Short-term politics won't leave sustainable childcare legacy. *Financial Review*. https://www.afr.com/politics/federal/short-term-politics-won-t-leave-sustainable-childcare-legacy-20240808-p5k0mz

Corscadden, L., Callander, E. J., & Topp, S. M. (2018). Disparities in access to health care in Australia for people with mental health conditions. *Australian Health Review*, *43*(6), 619–627.

Cortis, N., & Bullen, J. (2016). *Domestic violence and women's economic security: Building Australia's capacity for prevention and redress – Final report*. ANROWS & UNSW.

Coumarelos, C., Roberts, N., Weeks, N., & Rasmussen, V. (2023a). *Attitudes matter: The 2021 national community attitudes towards violence against women survey (NCAS), findings for young Australians*. ANROWS.

Coumarelos, C., Weeks, N., Bernstein, S., Roberts, N., Honey, N., Minter, K., & Carlisle, E. (2023b). *The 2011 national community attitudes towards violence against women survey (NCAS), findings for Australia*. ANROWS.

Council of Single Mothers and their Children. (2023). 'Single mother wins, then and now.' *CSMC*, 29 May. https://www.csmc.org.au/2023/05/29/single-mother-wins-then-and-now/

Cowan, S. (2017). *UBI: Universal basic income is an unbelievably bad idea*. Centre for Independent Studies.

Cox, E. (2019). Feminist perspectives on basic income. In E. Klein, J. Mays, & T. Dunlop (Eds.), *Implementing a basic income in Australia* (pp. 69–85). Palgrave Macmillan.

Crenshaw, K. (2017). *On intersectionality: Essential writings*. Columbia Law School.

Cripps, K. (2023). Indigenous women and intimate partner homicide in Australia: Confronting the impunity of policing failures. *Current Issues in Criminal Justice*, *35*(3), 293–311.

Crisp, P. (2022). *Undeserving instead of unfortunate: links between belief in meritocracy and low support for redistribution in Australia* [Master's thesis]. Erasmus Universiteit Rotterdam.

Cuesta, J. & Pico, J. (2020). The gendered poverty effects of the COVID-19 pandemic in Colombia. *The European Journal of Development Research*, *32*, 1558–1591.

Dahlberg, L., & Krug, E. (2002). Violence: A global public health problem. In E. Krug, L. Dahlberg, J. Mercy, A. Zwi, & R. Lozano (Eds.), *World report on violence and health*. World Health Organization.

Darab, S., & Hartman, Y. (2013). Understanding single older women's invisibility in housing issues in Australia. *Housing, Theory and Society*, *30*(4), 348–367.

Darab, S., Hartman, Y. & Holdsworth, L. (2018). What women want: Single older women and their housing preferences. *Housing Studies*, *33*(4), 525–543.

Davala, S., Jhabvala, R., Kapoor Mehta, S., & Standing, G. (2015). *Basic income: A transformative policy for India*. Bloomsbury.

Davala, S., Jhabvala, R., Standing, G., & Badgaiyan, N. (2017). *Piloting basic income a legacy study final report*. SEWA Bharat and INBI. Erişim Adresi, 26. https://www.scribd.com/document/507457499/Legacy-Study-Final-Report-a, 2020.

Davis, M. 2022. Speaking up: The truth about truth-telling. *Griffith Review*, (76): 25–35.

Deeming, C. (2013). The working class and welfare: Francis G. Castles on the political development of the welfare state in Australia and New Zealand thirty years on. *Social Policy & Administration*, *47*(6), 668–691.

Department of Health and Aged Care. (2025). *Medicare benefits schedule, item 80010*. https://www9.health.gov.au/mbs/fullDisplay.cfm?type=item&q=80010&qt=item

Department of Prime Minister & Cabinet (DPM&C). (2023). *Working together to deliver the NDIS – Independent review into the National Disability Insurance Scheme*. Commonwealth of Australia.

Department of Social Services (DSS). (2023a). *DSS benefit and payment recipient demographics – Quarterly data (June 2023)*. Australian Government. https://data.gov.au/data/dataset/dss-payment-demographic-data

Department of Social Services (DSS). (2023b). *Department of social services report: Evaluation of the EVP*. WhereTo Consulting.

Department of Social Services (DSS). (2024). *Expanded DSS benefit and payment recipient demographics – September 2024*. Australian Government. https://data.gov.au/dataset/ds-dga-cff2ae8a-55e4-47db-a66d-e177fe0ac6a0/distribution/dist-dga-fdbaedf6-70e9-4751-bb43-613bbc47e2c7/details?q=payment

de Paz-Báñez, M. A., Asensio-Coto, M. J., Sánchez-López, C., & Aceytuno, M. T. (2020). Is there empirical evidence on how the implementation of a universal basic income (UBI) affects labour supply? A systematic review. *Sustainability*, *12*(9459), 1–36.

de Souza, T. C. M. 2021. *The Bolsa Família case: A road to the unconditional basic income* (publication number 29097868) [M.P.S., Universidade NOVA de Lisboa (Portugal)]. ProQuest Dissertations & Theses Global.

Devereux, E. & Power, M. (2019). Fake news? A critical analysis of the 'welfare cheats, cheat us all' campaign in Ireland. *Critical Discourse Studies*, *16*(3), 347–362.

Dickinson, H., & Yates, S. (2023). A decade on: The achievements and challenges of The national disability insurance scheme's implementation. *Australian Journal of Social Issues*, *58*(3), 460–475.

Dudgeon, P., Blustein, S., Bray, A., Calma, T., McPhee, R. & Ring, I. (2021). *Connection between family, kinship and social and emotional wellbeing*. Austral ian Institute of Health & Welfare.

Dudgeon, P., & Walker, R. (2015). Decolonising Australian psychology: Discourses, strategies, and practice. *Journal of Social & Political Psychology*, *3*(1), 276–297.

Dudgeon, P., & Walker, R. (2022). An urgent call to address interpersonal and structural racism and social inequities in Australia. *The Lancet*, *400*, 2014–2016.

Dufty-Jones, R. (2017). A historical geography of housing crisis in Australia. *Australian Geographer*, *49*(1), 5–23.

Durnan, Z., & Inayatullah, S. (2020). From idea to reality: Universal basic income in Australia by 2030. *Journal of Future Studies*, *24*(3), 97–104.

Eatock, P. (1986). 'There's a snake in my caravan', In. Scutt, J.A. (Ed.) *Different lives: Reflections on the Women's Movement and Visions of its future*. Penguin Publishing.

Eatock, P. & Eatock, C. (2023). The personal is political, In. Arrow, M. (Ed.) *Women and Whitlam: revisiting the revolution*, pp. 56–74. Newsouth Publishing.

Edwards, T. (2023). Out of wedlock, out of luck: Single mothers and ex-nuptial babies, In. Arrow, M. (Ed.) *Women and Whitlam: Revisiting the revolution*, pp. 169–181. NewSouth Publishing.

Elson, D. (2017). Recognize, reduce, and redistribute unpaid care work: How to close the gender gap. *New Labor Forum*, *26*(2), 52–61.

Elster, J. (1986). Comment on van der Veen and van Parijs. *Theory & Society*, *15*(5), 709–721.

Enríquez, C. R. (2016). Basic income and time use democratization. *Basic Income Studies*, *11*(1), 39–48.

Esping-Andersen, G. (1990). *The three worlds of welfare capitalism*. Princeton University Press.

Evans, K. J., & Maley, J. F. (2020). Barriers to women in senior leadership: How unconscious bias is holding back Australia's economy. *Asia Pacific Journal of Human Resources*, *59*(2), 204–226.

Federici, S. (1975). *Wages against housework*. Power of Women Collective & Falling Wall Press. https://www.e-flux.com/legacy/2013/05/1.-Federici-Silvia-Wages-Against-Housework.pdf?b8c429

Fitzroy, F., & Jin, J. (2018). Basic income and public job offer: Complementary policies to reduce poverty and unemployment. *Journal of Poverty and Social Justice*, *26*(2), 191–206.

Flavel, J., McKee, M., Tesfay, F., Musolino, C., Freeman, T., van Eyk, H. & Baum, F. 2022. Explaining health inequalities in Australia: the contribution of income, wealth and employment. *Australian Journal of Primary Health*, *28*(6), 474–481.

Flood, M. (2019). Gender equality: Engaging men in change. *The Lancet*, *393*(10189), 2386–2387.

FoodBank Australia. (2024). *Hunger report 2024*. FoodBank Australia & Ipsos. https://reports.foodbank.org.au/wp-content/uploads/2024/10/2024_Foodbank_Hunger_Report_IPSOS-Report.pdf

Foley, M. & Cooper, R. (2021). Workplace gender equality in the post-pandemic era: Where to next? *Journal of Industrial Relations*, *64*(4), 463–476.

Fouksman, E., & Klein, E. (2019). Radical transformation or technological intervention? Two paths for universal basic income. *World Development*, *122*, 492–500.

Fraser, N. (1997). *Justice interruptus: Critical reflections on the 'postsocialist' condition*. Routledge.

Fraser, N. (2016). Contradictions of capital and care. *New Left Review*, (100). https://newleftreview.org/issues/ii100/articles/nancy-fraser-contradictions-of-capital-and-care

Fryer, B. (2024, July 22). *First Nations women are the fastest-growing group of people being sent to prison*. ABC News.

Fuller, K. (2024, June 26). *Mums tackling childcare waiting list stress gather their own data to put solutions on the table*. ABC News. https://www.abc.net.au/news/2024-06-26/families-facing-childcare-shortages-put-solutions-on-table/104016348

Garcia, M. (2021). *We are not born submissive: How patriarchy shapes women's lives*. Princeton University Press.

Gheaus, A. (2008). Basic income, gender justice and the costs of gender-symmetrical lifestyles. *Basic Income Studies*, *3*(3).

Gibson, M., Hearty, W., & Craig, P. (2020). The public health effects of interventions similar to basic income: A scoping review. *The Lancet Public Health*, *5*(3), E165–E176

Gibson, M., Stuart, J., Leske, S., Ward, R., & Tanton, R. (2021). Suicide rates for young Aboriginal and Torres Strait Islanders people: The influence of community level cultural connectedness. *Medical Journal of Australia*, *214*(11), 514–518.

Gil, D. (1981). The social context of domestic violence: Implications for prevention. *Vermont Law Review*, *6*, 339–362.

Gilley, T. (1991). *Empowering poor people – Research for action*. Melbourne.

Göker, Z. G. (2018). Gender, care, and welfare: Can caretakers allowances or basic income promote gender equality? *Journal of Women's Studies*, *19*(1), 115–130.

Goldblatt, B. (2022). Equal access to social and economic rights in Australia – the troubling case of ParentsNext. *Australian Journal of Human Rights*, *27*(3), 597–603.

Gonalons-Pons, P., & Calnitskyk, D. (2022). Exit, voice, and loyalty in the family: Findings from a basic income experiment. *Socio-Economic Review*, *20*(3), 1395–1423.

Goreng-Goreng, T. [Wakka Wakka]. (2017). Let's do something visionary in indigenous social policy. In T. Hollo (Ed.), *Views of a universal basic income* (pp. 5–8). The Green Institute. https://greens.org.au/sites/default/files/2020-07/lets-do-something-visionary-in-Indigenous-social-policy.pdf

Gould, C. (2025, February 13). *An eleventh hour rush to ram childcare changes through Senate — As it happened*. ABC News.

Greenstein, B. (2019). *Universal basic income may sound attractive but, if it occurred, would likelier increase poverty than reduce it*. Policy Futures – Centre on Budget and Policy Priorities. https://www.cbpp.org/sites/default/files/atoms/files/5-31-16bud.pdf

Grey, J. (2019). What could the Basic Income Guarantee do for women's rights? *Canadian Woman Studies Les Cahiers De La Femme*, *33*(1-2), 79–84.

Griffiths, R. 2017. No love on the dole: The influence of the UK means-tested welfare system on partnering and family structure. *Journal of Social Policy*, *46*(3), 543–561.

Guan, N., Guariglia, A., Moore, P., Xu, F., & Al-Janabi, H. (2022). Financial stress and depression in adults: A systematic review. *PLOS One*, *17*(2), 1–20.

Guerra, O., & Eboreime, E. (2021). The impact of economic recessions on depression, anxiety, and trauma-related disorders and illness outcomes – A scoping review. *Behavioural Sciences*, *11*(9), 1–41.

Hacker, J., Huber, G., Nichols, A., Rehm, P. Schlesinger, M., Valletta, R. & Craig, S. (2013). The economic security index: a new measure for research and policy analysis. *Review of Income and Wealth*, *60*(S1), S5–S32.

Hamer, L. & Tranter, K. (2021). Parents...Next: The ongoing neoliberalising of Australian social security. *Griffith Journal of Law and Human Dignity*, *9*(1), 29–55.

Hamilton, L. (2020). *Welfare doesn't work: The promises of basic income for a failed American safety net*. Palgrave Macmillan.

Hanna, R., & Olken, B. (2018). Universal basic income versus targeted transfers: Anti-poverty programs in developing countries. *Journal of Economic Perspectives, 32*(4), 201–226.

Harvey, D. (2007). *A brief history of neoliberalism*. Oxford University Press.

Hearn, J., Strid, S., Humbert, A. L., Balkmar, D., & Delaunay, M. (2022). From gender regimes to violence regimes: Re-thinking the position of violence. *Social Politics: International Studies in Gender, State & Society, 29*(2), 682–705.

Henderson, T. (2019). The principles, benefits, and politics of a basic income scheme for Australia. In P. Saunders (Ed.), *Revisiting Henderson: Poverty, social security, and basic income,* chapter 17. Melbourne University Publishing.

Henderson, T. 2021. *Basic income as a policy option for Australia* [PhD thesis]. University of Sydney. https://ses.library.usyd.edu.au/handle/2123/24536

Heron, R., Eisma, M., & Browne, K. (2020). Why do female domestic violence victims remain in or leave abusive relationships? A qualitative study. *Journal of Aggression, Maltreatment, & Trauma, 31*(5), 677–694.

Herscovitch, A. & Stanton, D. (2008). History of social security in Australia. *Family Matters,* (80), 51–60.

Hester, H., & Srnicek, N. (2023). *After work: A history of the home and the fight for free time*. Verso Trade.

Hill, N., Witt, K., Rajaram, G., McGorry, P., & Robinson, J. (2021). Suicide by young Australians, 2006-2015: A cross-sectional analysis of national coronial data. *The Medical Journal of Australia, 214*(3), 133–139.

Hocking, J. (2014). No Prime Minister changed Australia more than Gough Whitlam, *Monash Opinions,* 22 October. https://www.monash.edu/news/opinions/no-prime-minister-changed-australia-more-than-gough-whitlam

Hocking, J. (2018). A transforming sentiment in this country: the Whitlam government and Indigenous self-determination. *Australian Journal of Public Administration, 77*(S1), S5–S12.

Hollo, T. (2020, December 11). *58% of Australians support universal basic income!* The Green Institute Blog. https://www.greeninstitute.org.au/australians-support-universal-basic-income/

Holten, E. (2025). *Deficit: how feminist economics can change our world*. Penguin Random House.

Howard, M. W. (2015). Exploitation, labor and basic income. *Analyse & Kritik, 37*(1–2), 281–304.

Howard, N., Langridge, N., Mathur, V., Hamilton, L., Westlake, D., Soon-Shiong, N., Laker-Oketta, M., Davala, S., Martinez Tinaut, A., Lain, B. Morrow, V. & Franchi, M. (2024). *Doing radical things right: Ethical good practice for basic income experiments.* Centre for Development Studies, University of Bath.

Howard-Wagner, D., & Brown, C. (2021, August 6). *Increased incarceration of First Nations women is interwoven with the experience of violence and trauma.* The Conversation.

Howe, B. (2018a). Henderson's legacy: revisiting universal basic income. *Pursuit.* Available: https://pursuit.unimelb.edu.au/articles/henderson-s-legacy-revisiting-universal-basic-income?ct=t()

Howe, B. (2018b). Australians support universal health care, so why not a universal basic income? *The Conversation.* https://theconversation.com/australians-support-universal-health-care-so-why-not-a-universal-basic-income-91572

Howe, B. (2013). Social policy, In. Bramston, T. (Ed.) *The Whitlam Legacy*, chapter 19, pp. 282–299 Federation Press.

Howe, B. (2024). Reflections on making public policy (1977-1996). *Australian Journal of Social Issues*. https://doi.org/10.1002/ajs4.348

Howe, R. & Swain, S. (1993). Saving the child and punishing the mother: Single mothers and the state, 1912-1942. *Journal of Australian Studies, 17*(37), 31–46.

Hunter, B., Gray, M., & Crawford, H. (2016). *Who cares and does it matter for the labour market? A longitudinal analysis of the labour force status of Indigenous and non-Indigenous carers* (CAEPR Working Paper No. 106). Centre for Aboriginal Economic Policy Research, ANU.

Hurley, P., Matthews, H. & Pennicuik, S. (2022). *Deserts and oases: How accessible is childcare in Australia?* Victoria University.

Ingles, D., Philips, B., & Stewart, M. (2019). *A basic income for Australia? Exploring rationale, design, distribution, and cost*. Centre for Social Research Methods, ANU. https://csrm.cass.anu.edu.au/sites/default/files/docs/2019/10/BASIC_INCOME.pdf

International Committee of the Red Cross (ICRC). (2015). *What is economic security?* Retrieved November 12, 2024, from https://www.icrc.org/en/document/introduction-economic-security

International Labour Organization (ILO). (n.d.). *What we mean when we say 'economic security'*. Retrieved November 12, 2024, from https://webapps.ilo.org/public/english/protection/ses/download/docs/definition.pdf

International Labour Organization (ILO). (2018). *Care work and care jobs for the future of decent work*.

Irish Government. (2022). *Basic income for the arts pilot scheme: Guidelines*. https://www.gov.ie/en/publication/29337-basic-income-for-the-arts-pilot-scheme-guidelines-for-applicants/#

Isaacs, A. N., Enticott, J., Meadows, G., & Inder, B. (2018). Lower income levels in Australia are strongly associated with elevated psychological distress: Implications for healthcare and other policy areas. *Frontiers in Psychiatry, 9*(536), 1–9.

James, C. (2006). Winners and losers: The father factor in Australian child custody law in the 20th century. *Legal History, 10*, 207–238.

Jauch, H. (2015). The rise and fall of the basic income grant campaign: Lessons from Namibia. *Global Labour Journal, 6*(3), 336–350.

Jervis-Bardy, D. (2025, February 11). Australian billionaires face wealth tax under Greens' Robin Hood-style policies. *The Guardian*.

Johnson, M., Johnson, E., Nettle, D. & Pickett, K. 2022. Designing trials of universal basic income for health impact: Identifying interdisciplinary questions to address. *Journal of Public Health, 44*(2), 408–416.

Johnson, M. T., Johnson, E. A., Nettle, D., & Pickett, K. (2021). Designing trials of universal basic income for health impact: Identifying interdisciplinary questions to address. *Journal of Public Health, 44*(2), 408–416.

Jordan, S., Ferguson, G., & Haglin, K. (2021). Measuring and framing support for universal basic income. *Social Policy & Administration, 56*, 138–147.

Jordens, A. M. (1999). Australian Citizenship: Years of change. *Reform, 74*, 24–28.

Kandiyoti, D. (1988). Bargaining with patriarchy. *Gender and Society, 2*(3), 274–290.

Katada, K. (2014). Beyond the three selection principles of welfare policy (work, family, and belonging): toward a reconsideration of the Fujin Hogo Jigyo (Women's Protection Project) in Japan, In Vanderborght, Y. & Yamamoto, T. (Eds.) *Basic income in Japan*, pp. 101–114. Palgrave Macmillan.

Kawagoe, T. (2019). Experimental and game theoretical analyses of the unconditional basic income. In L. Delson (Ed.), *Empirical research on an unconditional basic income in Europe* (pp. 201–220). Springer.

Kelly, C. (2024, May 7). Melbourne private school students expelled over 'cruel' spreadsheet rating female classmates. *The Guardian*. https://www.theguardian.com/australia-news/article/2024/may/07/melbourne-private-school-students-expelled-over-cruel-spreadsheet-rating-female-classmates-yarra-valley-grammar-ntwnfb#:~:text=Two%20boys%20at%20a%20Melbourne,they%20had%20made%20the%20list

Kelsey-Sugg, A., & Hunt, S. (2024, September 25). *People caring for both children and elderly parents are on the rise; here's why 'sandwich carers' are struggling*. ABC News. https://www.abc.net.au/news/2024-09-25/sandwich-carers-invisible-labour-goes-unsupported/104369512

Kendall, G., Nguyen, H., & Ong, R. (2018). The association between income, wealth, economic security perception, and health: A longitudinal Australian study. *Health Sociology Review*, *28*(1), 20–38.

Kendall, G., Nguyen, H., & Ong, R. (2019). The association between income, wealth, economic security perception, and health: A longitudinal Australian study. *Health Sociology Review*, *28*(1), 20–38.

Kendall, S., Lighton, S., Sherwood, J., Baldry, E., & Sullivan, E. (2020). Incarcerated Aboriginal women's experiences of accessing healthcare and the limitations of the 'equal treatment' principle. *International Journal of Equity in Health*, *19*(48), 1–14.

Kerman, N. (2021). The role of universal basic income in preventing and ending homelessness. *International Journal on Homelessness, 1*(1), 3–13.

Ketterer, H. (2021). Living differently? A feminist-bourdieusian analysis of the transformative power of basic income. *The Sociological Review*, *69*(6), 1309–1324.

Klein, E. (2021a). Missing the value of care: When care is the focus of punitive welfare policy – ParentsNext. *Arena,* (6), 43–48.

Klein, E. (2021b). Unpaid care, welfare conditionality, and expropriation. *Gender, Work & Organization*, *28*(4), 1475–2489.

Klein, E., Cook, K., Maury, S., & Bowey, K. (2022a). An exploratory study examining the changes to Australia's social security system during COVID-19 lockdown measures. *Australian Journal of Social Issues*, *57*(1), 51–69.

Klein, E., Cook, K., Maury, S., & Bowey, K. (2022b). Understanding COVID-19 emergency social security measures as a form of basic income: lessons from Australia. *Journal of Sociology*, *59*(4), 879–893.

Klein, E., Hunt, J., Staines, Z., Dinku, Y., Brown, C., Glynn-Braun, K., & Yap, M. (2024). *Caring about care*. Australian National University & Australian Human Rights Commission.

Klein, E., Mays, J., & Dunlop, T. (2019). *Implementing a basic income in Australia*. Palgrave Macmillan.

Kleinman, A. (2012). The art of medicine. Caregiving as moral experience. *The Lancet*, *380*(3), 1550–1551.

Korpi, W. & Palme, J. (1998). The paradox of redistribution and strategies of equality: welfare state institutions, inequality, and poverty in the Western countries. *American Sociological Review, 63*(5), 661–687.

Koslowski, A., & Duvander, A. Z. (2018). Basic income: The potential for gendered empowerment? *Social Inclusion, 6*(4), 8–15.

Kowalska, M. (2023). Impact of the unconditional basic income on the professional situation of women. *Financial Internet Quarterly, 19*(2), 18–25.

Krakouer, M. [Mineng Noongar]. (2020, October 2). A universal wage will reduce poverty for First Nations people and for all Australians. *Independent Australia*. https://independentaustralia.net/australia/australia-display/a-universal-wage-will-reduce-poverty-for-first-nations-people-and-for-all-australians,14365

Kuipers, Y. J., van Beeck, E., Cijsouw, A., & van Gils, Y. (2021). The impact of motherhood on the course of women's psychological wellbeing. *Journal of Affective Disorders Reports, 6*, 1–8.

Kutin, J., Russell, R., & Reid, M. (2017). Economic abuse between intimate partners in Australia: Prevalence, health status, disability and financial stress. *Australian and New Zealand Journal of Public Health, 41*(4), 269–274.

Lakoff, G. (2004). *Don't think of an elephant*. Chelsea Green Publishing.

Langridge, N. (2024). Unconditional basic income and a degrowth transition: Adding empirical rigour to radical visions. *Futures, 159*, 103375): 1–14.

Lapine, C., Sachdev, A. R., & Vaghani, S. (2021). Basic income: How to help women and reduce gender disparity. *Industrial and Organizational Psychology, 14*(4), 593–596.

Lazar, O. (2020). Work, domination and the false hope of universal basic income. *Res Publica, 27*(3), 427–446.

Lee, D., & Craig, L. (2024). Australian Parental leave policy, employers' cognitive bias, and mothers' wages: Penalty or premium? *Gender, Work & Organization*. https://doi.org/10.1111/gwao.13216

Levasseur, K., Paterson, S., & Nathalia Carvalho, M. (2018). Conditional and unconditional cash transfers: Implications for gender. *Basic Income Studies, 13*(1): 1–9.

Lewis, M. & Lee, A. (2020). Affording health during the COVID-19 pandemic and associated economic downturn. *Australian New Zealand Journal of Public Health, 44*(6), 519–520.

Lombardozzi, L. (2020). Gender inequality, social reproduction and the universal basic income. *The Political Quarterly, 91*(2), 317–323.

Luccioni, L. (2020). UBI activism in Australia: The present. In R. Caputo & L. Liu (Eds.), *Political activism and basic income guarantee* (pp. 163–184). Springer, Palgrave Macmillan.

Luterman, S. (2022, August 30). Magnolia Mother's Trust marks a history-making three cycles of paying back mothers $1,000 a month. *Next City*. https://nextcity.org/urbanist-news/magnolia-mothers-trust-marks-a-history-making-three-cycles-of-paying-black

Maher, J., Fitz-Gibbon, K., Meyer, S., Roberts, S., & Pfitzner, N. (2021). Mothering through and in violence: Discourses of the 'good mother'. *Sociology, 55*(4), 659–676.

Makole, K. R., Ntshangase, B. A., Maringa, M. S., & Msosa, S. K. (2022). Can a basic income grant improve the quality of life for the poor in South Africa: An analytical review. *Business Ethics and Leadership, 6*(3), 57–67.

Marston, G. (2019). Basic income in Australia: Implementation challenges. In. Klein, E., Mays, J., & Dunlop, T. (Eds.) *Implementing a basic income in Australia: pathways forward*, pp. 23–43. Palgrave Macmillan.

Marston, G., Humpage, L., Peterie, M., Mendes, P., Bielefeld, S. & Staines, Z. (2022). *Compulsory income management in Australia and New Zealand: more harm than good?* Policy Press.

Marston, G., & Peterie, M. (2020). Is universal basic income a desirable alternative to conditional welfare? *Social Alternatives*, *39*(1), 39–46.

Marston, G., & Staines, Z. (2019). Social policy. In. Barry, N., Chen, P., Haigh, Y., Motta, S. & Perche, D. (Eds.), *Australian politics and policy*, pp. 547–559. Sydney University Press.

Marston, G., & Staines, Z. (2020). Losing sight: Social security policy in Australia, In. McClelland, D. et al. (Eds.) *Social Policy in Australia: Understanding for Action* (4th ed.), pp. 214–237. Oxford University Press.

Martin, S., Schofield, T., & Butterworth, P. (2022). News media representations of people receiving income support And the production of stigma power: An empirical Analysis of reporting on two Australian welfare payments. *Critical Social Policy*, *42*(4), 648–670.

Mays, J., & Marston, G. (2016). Reimagining equity and egalitarianism: The basic income debate in Australia. *Journal of Sociology and Social Welfare*, *43*, 9–25.

McDonald, J. & Spindler, Z.A. (1988). Benefit-induced female sole parenthood in Australia, 1973-1985. *Australian Economic Papers*, *27*(50), 1–19.

McKeever, G., & Walsh, T. (2020). The moral hazard of conditionality: Restoring the integrity of social security law. *Australian Journal of Social Issues*, *55*(1), 73–87.

McKinley, C. E., Liddell, J., & Lilly, J. (2021). All work and no play: Indigenous women 'pulling the weight' in home life. *Social Service Review*, *95*(2), 278–311.

McLean, C. (2016). …and justice for all? Basic income and the principles of gender equality. *Juncture*, *22*(4), 284–288.

McQuire, A. (2018, November 26). *We can't dismantle systems of violence unless we centre Aboriginal women*. IndigenousX. https://indigenousx.com.au/we-cant-dismantle-systems-of-violence-unless-we-centre-aboriginal-women/

McQuire, A., Watego, C., Singh, D., & Strakosch, E. (2023, March 30). *What happened to the Senate Inquiry into missing and murdered indigenous women?* The Conversation.

Meadows, G. N., Enticott, J. C., Inder, B., Russell, G. M., & Gurr, R. (2015). Better access to mental health care and the failure of the Medicare principle of universality. *Medical Journal of Australia*, *202*(4), 190–194.

Melbourne Institute. (2023a). *Poverty lines: Australia: March Quarter, 2023*. University of Melbourne. https://melbourneinstitute.unimelb.edu.au/__data/assets/pdf_file/0003/4710153/Poverty-Lines-Australia-March-Quarter-2023.pdf

Melbourne Institute. (2023b). *Poverty lines: December quarter, 2023*. University of Melbourne. https://melbourneinstitute.unimelb.edu.au/__data/assets/pdf_file/0005/4930898/Poverty-Lines-Australia-December-Quarter-2023.pdf

Méndez, S., Scott, A., & Zhang, Y. (2022). Improving access to health care in Australia. In P. Dawkins & A. Payne (Eds.), *Economic and social policy: Towards evidence-based policy solutions*, chapter 6. University of Melbourne.

Meyer, S. (2011). Seeking help for intimate partner violence: Victims' experiences when approaching the criminal justice system for IPV-related support and protection in an Australian jurisdiction. *Feminist Criminology*, *6*(4), 268–290.

Meyer, S. (2012). Why women stay: A theoretical examination of rational choice and moral reasoning in the context of intimate partner violence. *Journal of Criminology*, *45*(2), 179–193.

Meyerson, D., & Fletcher, J. (2000). A modern manifesto for shattering the glass ceiling. *Harvard Business Review*. https://hbr.org/2000/01/a-modest-manifesto-for-shattering-the-glass-ceiling

Miller, A., Yamamori, T., & Zelleke, A. (2023). The gender effects of basic income. In M. Torry (Ed.), *The Palgrave Macmillan international handbook of basic income*, chapter 9. Springer Nature.

Milligan, K. (2016). *Dare to dream, but do the math*. CD Howe Institute. https://cdhowe.org/publication/kevin-milligan-dare-dream-do-math/

Moreton-Robinson, A. (2000). *Talkin' up to the white woman: Indigenous women and feminism*. University of Queensland Press.

Moreton-Robinson, A. (2009). Imagining the good Indigenous citizen: Race war and the pathology of patriarchal white sovereignty. *Cultural Studies Review*, *15*(2), 61–79.

Moreton-Robinson, A. (2015). *The white possessive: Property, power, and indigenous sovereignty*. University of Minnesota Press.

Morini, C. (2021). Life is mine: Feminism, self-determination, and basic income. *Radical Philosophy*, *209*, 75–80.

Morley, C., Ablett, P., & Mays, J. (2019). Universal basic income: What difference might it make? *Social Alternatives*, *38*(2), 11–18.

Morris, A. (2023, August 8). *"It's soul destroying": How people on a housing wait list of 175,00 describe their years of waiting*. The Conversation. https://theconversation.com/its-soul-destroying-how-people-on-a-housing-wait-list-of-175-000-describe-their-years-of-waiting-210705

Morris, A., Robinson, C., & Idle, J. (2022, August 5). *'I left with the kids and ended up homeless with them': The nightmare of housing wait lists for people fleeing domestic violence*. The Conversation. https://theconversation.com/i-left-with-the-kids-and-ended-up-homeless-with-them-the-nightmare-of-housing-wait-lists-for-people-fleeing-domestic-violence-187687

Morrison, S. (2015). *Address to the National Press Club: The best form of welfare*. Australian Government. https://formerministers.dss.gov.au/15959/address-to-the-national-press-club-the-best-form-of-welfare/

Murphy, J. (2024). *An unlikely survival: The politics of welfare in Australia since 1950*. Melbourne University Press.

Muthalaly, R., Nelson, A., Baradi, A., Mehta, O., Wilson, A., & Nasis, A. (2023). Socioeconomic determinants of health, traditional risk factors and cardiovascular outcomes in Australia. *International Journal of Cardiology, Cardiovascular Risk and Prevention*, *17*, 1–7.

O'Connor, B. (2001). The intellectual origins of 'welfare dependency'. *Australian Journal of Social Issues*, *36*(3), 221–236.

O'Loughlin, K., Browning, C., & Kendig, H. (2017). *Ageing in Australia: Challenges and opportunities*. Springer.

O'Neill, M. & Johns, R. (2009). The history of welfare and paid maternity leave in Australia, *Proceedings of the IERA Conference, 2009*. https://opus.lib.uts.edu.au/bitstream/10453/11435/1/2009001270OK.pdf

Onifade, E., Shishane, K., Elonge, F., & Glover, L. (2023). Guaranteed income: Experiences of African American mothers in the Magnolia Mother's Trust Project. *University of Bedfordshire*. https://uobrep.openrepository.com/handle/10547/625900

O'Reilly, A. (2010). *Twenty-first century motherhood: experience, identity, policy, agency*. Columbia University Press.

Organization for Economic Cooperation Development (OECD). 2024. *Social expenditure database, updated 24 June 2024*. Retrieved November 12, 2024, from https://web-archive.oecd.org/temp/2024-06-24/63248-expenditure.htm

Our Watch. (2025). *Our Watch: Quick facts*. https://www.ourwatch.org.au/quick-facts/

Parfitt, C., & Barnes, T. (2020). Rethinking economic security in a precarious world. *Critical Sociology*, *46*(4–5), 487–494.

Pateman, C. (2004). Democratizing citizenship: Some advantages of a basic income. *Politics & Society*, *32*(1), 89–105.

Paterson, N., & Farrugia, C. (2020). *Experiences of food insecurity for Australian women and children affected by domestic and family violence*. Australian Institute of Family Studies (AIFS).

Patulny, R., & Spies-Butcher, B. (2023). Come together? The unusual combination of precariat materialist and educated post-materialist support for an Australian universal basic income. *Journal of Sociology*, *59*(4), 2023.

Patwardhan, V., Gil, G., Arrieta, A., Cagney, J., DeGraw, E., Herbert, M., Khalil, M., Mullany, E., O'Connell, E., Spencer, C., Stein, C., Valikhanova, A., Gakidou, E., & Flor, L. (2024). Differences across the lifespan between females and males in the top 20 causes of disease burden globally: A systematic analysis of the global burden of disease study 2021. *Lancet Public Health*, *9*(5): E282–E294.

Peachment, A. (1976). Experiments in decision-making: the Whitlam legacy. *Journal of Commonwealth & Comparative Politics*, *14*(3), 273–285.

Pearson, N. (2014). Noel Pearson's eulogy for Gough Whitlam in full. *Sydney Morning Herald*. https://www.smh.com.au/opinion/noel-pearsons-eulogy-for-gough-whitlam-in-full-20141105-11haeu.html

Pennington, A., & Stanford, J. (2020). *Gender inequality in Australia's labour market: A factbook*. The Australia Institute, Centre for Future Work.

People with Disability Australia (PWDA). (2023). *Disability and poverty*. PWDA. https://pwd.org.au/wp-content/uploads/2023/02/PWDASB-2023-Extent-and-Nature-of-Poverty.pdf

Pereira, R. (Ed.). (2023). *Financing basic income: A dual income proposal*. Palgrave.

Petrie, K., Baldwin, P., Crawford, J., & Harvey, S. (2021). The voice of mental health practice in Australia: A mixed-method cross-sectional study of gaps and areas of need. *Australia and New Zealand Journal of Public Health*, *45*(4), 318–324.

Pfutze, T., & Rodriguez-Castelan, C. (2019). Can a small social pension promote labor force participation? Evidence from the Colombia mayor program. *Economia Journal*, (Fall 2019), 111–154.

Phillips, B. (2018). *Research note: modelling a basic income for Australia – Simple example of a universal pension funded by increased personal income taxation*. ANU Centre for Social Research and Methods. https://csrm.cass.anu.edu.au/sites/default/files/docs/CSRM_Research_Note_Basic_Income_final.pdf

Phillips, B., Gray, M. & Biddle, N. (2020). *Covid-19 JobKeeper and JobSeeker impacts on poverty and housing stress under current and alternative economic and policy scenarios.* Centre for Social Research & Methods, Australian National University. https://openresearch-repository.anu.edu.au/bitstream/1885/213186/1/Impact_of_Covid19_JobKeeper_and_Jobeeker_measures_on_Poverty_and_Financial_Stress_FINAL.pdf

Piachaud, D. (2018). Basic income: Confusion, claims and choices. *Journal of Poverty and Social Justice*, *26*(3), 299–314.

Piketty, T. (2014). *Capital in the twenty-first century.* Harvard University Press.

Pin, L., Levac, L., & Rodenburg, E. (2023). Legislated poverty? An intersectional policy analysis of COVID-19 income support programs in Ontario, Canada. *Journal of Poverty*, *27*(5), 404–425.

Pocock, B., Elton, J., Preston, A., Charlesworth, S., MacDonald, F., Baird, M., Cooper, R., & Ellem, B. (2008). The impact of 'work choices' on women in low paid employment in Australia: A qualitative analysis. *Journal of Industrial Relations*, *50*(3), 475–488.

Poelina, A., Perdrisat, M., Wooltorton, S., & Lee Mulligan, E. (2023). Feeling and hearing country as research method. *Environmental Education Research*, *29*(10), 1486–1501.

Prabhakar, R. (2020). Universal basic income and Covid-19. *IPPR Progressive Review*, *17*(1), 105–113.

Productivity Commission. 2024. *A path to universal early childhood education and care – Inquiry report.* Australian Government. https://www.pc.gov.au/inquiries/completed/childhood/report

Quiggin, J., Klein, E., Dunlop, T., Henderson, T., & Goodall, J. (2020a). *Liveable income guarantee: Working paper.* Tax and Transfer Policy Institute, Crawford School of Public Policy, Australian National University. https://apo.org.au/node/308260

Quiggin, J., Klein, E., & Henderson, T. (2020b, October 1). *Meet the liveable income guarantee: A budget-ready proposal that would prevent unemployment benefits falling off a cliff.* The Conversation.

Rahardja, G. (2024, July 10). *Two years after the launch of a public transport safety tol, advocates say harassment is still going unreported.* ABC News. https://www.abc.net.au/news/2024-07-10/women-public-transport-safety-sexual-assault-victoria/104070092

Raynor, K. & Panza, L. (2021). Tracking the impact of COVID-1i in Victoria, Australia: Shocks, vulnerability and insurances among residents of share houses. *Cities*, *117*, 1–12.

Recalde, M. & Vesterlund, L. (2023). Gender differences in negotiation: Can interventions reduce the gap? *Annual Review of Economics*, *15*, 633–657.

Regan, S. (2014). *Australia's welfare system: a review of reviews, 1941–2013.* Australian National University.

Regan, S. & Stanton, D. (2019). The Henderson poverty inquiry in context, In. Saunders, P. (Ed.) *Revisiting Henderson: poverty, social security, and basic income*, Chapter 3, pp. 47–66 Melbourne University Publishing.

Reid, E. (2023). *Revolution and reform: the women's liberation movement and the Whitlam years* https://static1.squarespace.com/static/58c4509d9dc4bbecc7737bc3/t/64ec3986d1e6412dc0966d8a/1693202830566/Elizabeth+Reid+Whitlam+Legacy+Paper+-+Revolution+and+Reform.pdf

Riches, C., & North, A. (2024). 'Why are so many neurodivergent women misdiagnosed?' *Insights,* Australian Psychological Association. https://psychology.org.au/insights/why-are-so-many-neurodivergent-women-misdiagnosed

Ridley, M., Rao, G., Schilbach, F., & Patel, V. (2020). Poverty, depression, and anxiety: Causal evidence and mechanisms. *Science*, *370*(6522), 1–12.

Roebyns, I. (2000). Hush money or emancipation fee? A gender analysis of basic income. In R. van der Veen & L. Grott (Eds.), *Basic income on the agenda: Policy objectives and political chances* (pp. 121–136). Amsterdam University Press.

Rohde, N., Ki Tang, K., Osberg, L., & Rao, D. S. P. (2015). Economic insecurity in Australia: Who is feeling the pinch and how? *Economic Record*, *91*(292), 1–15.

Rohde, N., Tang, K., Osberg, L., & Rao, P. (2016). The effect of economic insecurity on mental health: Recent evidence from Australian panel data. *Social Science & Medicine*, *151*, 250–258.

Rohde, N., Tang, K., Osberg, L., & Rao, P. (2017). Is it vulnerability or economic insecurity that matters for health? *Journal of Economic Behaviour and Organization*, *134*, 307–319.

Rottenberg, C. (2022). Women who work: The limits of The neoliberal feminist paradigm. In P. Maclaran, L. Stevens, & O. Kravets (Eds.), *The Routledge companion to marketing and feminism*. Routledge.

Royal Commission into Aged Care Quality and Safety. (2021). *Final report: Care, dignity, and respect*. Australian Government.

Royal Commission on Human Relationships. (1974). *Final reports*. Australian Government. https://apo.org.au/node/34438

Ruckert, A., Huynh, C., & Labonté, R. (2018). Reducing health inequities: Is universal basic income the way forward? *Journal of Public Health*, *40*(1), 3–7.

Sabbioni, J. (1996). Aboriginal women's narratives. *Australian Historical Studies*, *27*(106), 72–78.

Samuel, S. (2020). *Everywhere basic income has been tried, in one map*. https://www.vox.com/future-perfect/2020/2/19/21112570/universal-basic-income-ubi-map

Saunders, P. (1981). The Committee of Inquiry into Poverty's Guaranteed Minimum Income Scheme: A Perspective from the 1980's. *The Australian Economic Review*, *14*, 20–28.

Saunders, P. (2004). What is fair about a 'fair go'. *Policy*, *20*(1), 3–10.

Saunders, P. (Ed.) (2019). *Revisiting Henderson: poverty, social security and basic income*. Melbourne University Publishing.

Sawer, M. (2023). Part one: women and political influence – Introduction, In. Arrow, M. (Ed.) *Women and Whitlam: revisiting the revolution*, Part 1, pp. 3–7. NewSouth Publishing.

Schulz, P. (2017). Universal basic income in a feminist perspective and gender analysis. *Global Social Policy, 17*(1), 89–92.

Services Australia. (2023a). *About Medicare*. Australian Government. https://www.servicesaustralia.gov.au/about-medicare?context=60092

Services Australia. (2023b). *Mental health and Medicare*. https://www.servicesaustralia.gov.au/mental-health-care-and-medicare?context=60092

Services Australia. (2024a). *Medicare and tax*. Australian Government. https://www.servicesaustralia.gov.au/medicare-and-tax?context=60092

Services Australia. (2024b). *Your income can affect Childcare Subsidy*. https://www.servicesaustralia.gov.au/your-income-can-affect-child-care-subsidy?context=41186

Services Australia. (2024c). *ParentsNext*. Australian Government. https://www.servicesaustralia.gov.au/parentsnext

Services Australia. (2024d). *Parent Pathways*. Australian Government. https://www.servicesaustralia.gov.au/parent-pathways

Sharma, M. & Rawal, S. (2022). Women in medicine: the limits of individualism in academic medicine. *Academic Medicine*, *97*(3), 346–350.

Shattell, M. (2017). Work-life balance: Slow down, move, and think. *Journal of Psychosocial Nursing and Mental Health Services*, *55*(3), 13–14.

Shaver, S. (1987). Design for a welfare state: The joint parliamentary committee on social security. *Historical Studies*, *22*(88), 411–431.

Sheared, V. (1998). *Race, gender, and welfare reform*. Routledge

Singh, S. (2020). Economic abuse and family violence across cultures: Gendering money and assets through coercive control. In M. McMahon, & P. McGorrery (Eds.), *Criminalising coercive control: Family violence and the criminal law* (pp. 51–72). Springer.

Sleep, L. (2019). *Domestic violence, social security and the couple rule. ANROWS Research Report*, *4*. https://anrows.intersearch.com.au/anrowsjspui/bitstream/1/18659/1/RP_17_02_Sleep_D_RR_social-security_couple-rule.pdf

Sleep, L. (2023). Female dependents, individual customers, and promiscuous digital personas: The multiple governing of women through The Australian social security couple rule. *Critical Social Policy*, *43*(2), 193–213.

Sloman, P., Zamora Vargas, D., & Ramos Pinto, P. (2019). Introduction. In P. Sloman, D. Zamora Vargas, & P. Ramos Pinto (Eds.), *Universal basic income in historical perspective* (pp. 1–16). Palgrave Macmillan.

Sloman, P., Zamora Vargas, D., & Ramos Pinto, P. (Eds.). (2019). *Universal basic income in historical perspective*. Palgrave Macmillan.

Smith, J. (2017). Paying for care in Australia's 'wage earners' welfare state: The case of child endowment. In M. Stewart (Ed.), *Tax, social policy and gender: Rethinking equality and efficiency* (pp. 161–205). ANU Press.

Smyth, P. (2012). Securing the social conditions for individual autonomy in Australia. *Australian Social Work*, *65*(1), 1–5.

Sobeck, K. and Breunig, R. (2023). 'How removing parenting payments when children turned 8 harmed rather than helped single mothers.' *The Conversation*. https://theconversation.com/how-removing-parenting-payments-when-children-turned-8-harmed-rather-than-helped-single-mothers-204927

Soss, J., Fording, R., & Schram, S. (2011). *Disciplining the poor: Neoliberal paternalism and the persistent power of race*. University of Chicago Press.

Spies-Butcher, B. (2018). *Basic income as a progressive priority*. The Australia Institute. https://australiainstitute.org.au/wp-content/uploads/2020/12/Basic_Income_Symposium_Spies-Butcher_final.pdf

Spies-Butcher, B., & Henderson, T. (2019). Stepping stones to an Australian basic income. In E. Klein, J. Mays, & T. Dunlop (Eds.), *Implementing a basic income in Australia: Exploring the basic income guarantee* (pp. 163–178). Palgrave Macmillan.

Spies-Butcher, B., Phillips, B., & Henderson, T. (2020). Between universalism and targeting: Exploring policy pathways for an Australian basic income. *The Economic and Labour Relations Review*, *31*(4), 502–523.

Srnicek, N. & Williams, A. 2015. *Inventing the future: Postcapitlism and a world without work*. Verso.

Staines, Z. (2018). Ground-level impacts of remote employment policy: Social disadvantage under the Community Development Programme. *Journal of Australian Political Economy*, *82*, 107–132.

Staines, Z. (2021). Australia's remote workfare policy: Rhetoric versus reality of 'community' empowerment. *Critical Social Policy*, *41*(1), 4–24.

Staines, Z. (2022, December 12). *Tackling gender-based inequality at the nexus of employment, social security, and care: What next for women?* Power to Persuade. https://www.powertopersuade.org.au/blog/tackling-gender-based-inequality-at-the-nexus-of-employment-social-security-and-care-what-next-for-women/12/12/2022

Staines, Z. (2023). Work and wellbeing in remote Australia: Moving beyond punitive 'workfare'. *Journal of Sociology*, *59*(4), 808–827.

Staines, Z. (2025). *A UBI for Australia? A nationally representative survey of Australians' views on UBI*. The University of Queensland.

Staines, Z., Altman, J., Klein, E., & Markham, F. (2021a). *Remote access: Guiding principles for a new livelihood and work program in remote Indigenous Australia*. The Australia Institute. https://australiainstitute.org.au/wp-content/uploads/2021/08/P1124-Guiding-principles-for-a-new-livelihood-and-work-program-in-remote-Indigenous-Australia-Web.pdf

Staines, Z., Marston, G., Bielefeld, S., Humpage, L., Mendes, P. & Peterie, M. (2021b). Governing poverty: Compulsory income management and crime in Australia. *Critical Criminology*, *29*, 745–761.

Staines, Z., Marston, G., Peterie, M., Bielefeld, S., Mendes, P., & Roche, S. (2024). An intersectional feminist analysis of compulsory income management in Australia. *Journal of Social Policy*. https://doi.org/10.1017/S0047279424000205

Staines, Z., & Smith, K. (2022). Workfare and food in remote Australia: 'I haven't eaten… I'm really at the end…'. *Critical Policy Studies*, *16*(1), 36–59.

Staines, Z., & Zahnow, R. (2022). Exploring the politics of strain: Crime and welfare in remote indigenous Australia. *Social Policy & Administration*, *56*(3), 452–471.

Stambe, R., & Marston, G. (2023). Checking activation at the door: Rethinking the welfare-work nexus in light of Australia's COVID-19 response. *Social Policy & Society*, *22*(1), 106–121.

Standing, G. (2011). *The precariat: The new dangerous class*. Bloomsbury Academic.

Standing, G. (2015). *Basic income: And how we can make it happen*. Penguin Press.

Standing, G. (2017). *Basic income and how we can make it happen*. Penguin Press.

Stanford, J., Macdonald, F., & Raynes, L. (2022). *Collective bargaining and wage growth in Australia*. The Australia Institute, Centre for Future Work.

Stephens, R. (2019). The universal basic income: Should it replace the existing social security system? *Policy Quarterly*, *15*(1), 30–37.

Stewart, M. (Ed.). (2017). *Tax, social policy and gender: Rethinking equality and efficiency* (pp. 161–205). ANU Press.

Summers, A. (2022). *The choice: Violence or poverty – Domestic violence and its consequences in Australia today*. University of Technology.

Temple, J., Booth, S., & Pollard, C. (2019). Social assistance payments and food insecurity in Australia: Evidence from the household expenditure survey. *International Journal of Environmental Research and Public Health*, *16*(3), 1–15.

Ter-Minassian, T. (2020). Financing A universal basic income: A primer. In U. Gentilini, M. Grosh, J. Rigolini, & R. Yemtsov (Eds.), *Exploring universal basic income: A guide to navigating concepts, evidence, and practices, chapter 5* (pp. 153–182). World Bank Group.

The Greens. (2022). *Policy initiative – No poverty in a wealth country, a liveable income guaranteed for all* The Greens.

The Greens. (2025). *Restore the CES: Greens will abolish for-profit job services and end mutual obligations.* https://greens.org.au/news/media-release/restore-ces-greens-will-abolish-profit-job-services-and-end-mutual-obligations

The Green Institute. (2020). *58% of Australians support universal basic income!* https://www.greeninstitute.org.au/australians-support-universal-basic-income/

Thompson, M. (2022). Money for everything? Universal basic income in a crisis. *Economy & Society*, *51*(3), 353–374.

Uhde, Z. (2018). Caring revolutionary transformation: Combined effects of a universal basic income and public model of care. *Basic Income Studies*, *13*(2), 1–12.

Ulmestig, R., & Eriksson, M. (2016). Financial consequences of leaving violent men – Women survivors of domestic violence and the social assistance system in Sweden. *European Journal of Social Work*, *20*(4), 560–571.

UNDP. (2021, March 4). *UNDP calls for temporary basic income to help world's poorest women cope with effects of COVID-19 pandemic.* UNDP News. https://www.undp.org/press-releases/undp-calls-temporary-basic-income-help-worlds-poorest-women-cope-effects-covid-19-pandemic

United Nations. (2020). *The world's women 2020: Trends and statistics.* https://worlds-women-2020-data-undesa.hub.arcgis.com/

United Nations Development Programme (UNDP). (2018). *Now is the time! Reduce and redistribute the unpaid domestic and care work burden of women for sustainable development.* https://www.undp.org/sites/g/files/zskgke326/files/migration/asia_pacific_rbap/RBAP-Gender-2018-Now-is-the-Time.pdf

van der Veen, R. J., & van Parijs, P. (1986). A capitalist road to communism. *Theory & Society*, *15*(5), 635–655.

Van Parijs, P. (1997). *Real freedom for all: What (if anything) can justify capitalism?* Oxford University Press.

Van Parijs, P. (2004). Basic income: A simple and powerful idea for the twenty-first century. *Politics & Society*, *32*(1), 7–39.

Van Parijs, P., & Vanderborght, Y. (2017). *Basic income: A radical proposal for A free society and A sane economy.* Harvard University Press.

Vidojević, J. & Chipkin, I. (2021). The gendered character of welfare: reconsidering vulnterability and violence in South Africa. *Social Dynamics: A Journal of African Studies*, *47*(3), 472–487.

Vogel, J. P., Jung, J., Lavin, T., Simpson, G., Kluwgant, D., Abalos, E., Diaz, V., Downe, S., Filippi, V., Gallos, I., Galadanci, H., Katageri, G., Homer, C., Hofmeyr, J., Liabsuetrakul, T., Morhason-Bello, I., Osoti, A., Souza, J.P., Thakar, R. […] & Oladapo, O. (2024). Neglected medium-term and long-term consequences of labour and childbirth: A systematic analysis of the burden, recommended practices and a way forward. *Lancet Global Health*, *12*(2): E317–E330.

Vollenweider, C. (2017). Domestic service and gender equality: An unavoidable problem for the feminist debate on basic income. *Basic Income Studies*, *8*(1), 19–41.

Wacquant, L. (2009). *Punishing the poor: The neoliberal government of social insecurity.* Duke University Press.

Walby, S. (2009). *Globalization and inequalities.* Sage.

Walters, M. (2002). Labour market participation and the married to sole mother transition. In Eardley, T., & Bradbury, B. (Eds.), *Competing visions*, pp. 411–421. University of New South Wales.

Wang, J., Lloyd-Evans, B., Giacco, D., Forsyth, R., Nebo, C., Mann, F. & Johnson, S. (2017). Social isolation in mental health: a conceptual and methodological review. *Social Psychiatric Epidemiology*, *52*(12), 1451–1461.

Warren, T. (2010). Work time. Leisure time. On women's temporal and economic wellbeing in Europe. *Community, Work & Family*, *13*(4), 365–392.

Watson, K., & Ritchie, H. (2024, April 29). *Australians call for tougher laws on violence against women after killings.* BBC News. https://www.bbc.com/news/world-australia-68915018

Weeks, K. (2020). Anti-postwork feminist politics and a case for basic income. *Communication, Capitalism and Critique, 18*(2), 575–594.

Weeks, K. (2011). *The problem with work: Feminism, marxism, antiwork politics, and postwork imaginaries.* Duke University Press.

Weller, C. & Logan, A. (2009). Measuring middle class economic security. *Journal of Economic Issues, XLIII*(2), 327–336.

WGEA. (2018). *Gender and negotiation in the workplace.* Australian Government. https://www.wgea.gov.au/sites/default/files/documents/Negotiation-Paper-Final_0.pdf

WGEA. (2019). *Gender segregation in Australia's workforce.* Australian Government. https://www.wgea.gov.au/publications/gender-segregation-in-australias-workforce#gender-seg-industry

WGEA. (2024). *Gender pay gap data.* Australian Government. https://www.wgea.gov.au/pay-and-gender/gender-pay-gap-data

Widerquist, K. (2018). *A critical analysis of basic income experiments for researchers, policymakers, and citizens.* Springer.

Widerquist, K. (2024). *Universal basic income.* MIT Press.

Wilcock, S. (2014). Official discourses of the Australian 'welfare cheat'. *Current Issues in Criminal Justice*, *26*(2), 177–194.

Wolf, S. & Willis, C. (2018). *Universal basic income as a tool of empowerment for minorities.* European Centre for Minority Issues.

Wolfe, P. (2006). Settler colonialism and the elimination of the native. *Journal of Genocide Research*, *8*(4), 387–409.

Wood, D., Griffiths, K., & Crowley, T. (2021). *Women's work: The impact of The COVID crisis on Australian women.* Grattan Institute. https://grattan.edu.au/wp-content/uploads/2021/03/Womens-work-Grattan-Institute-report.pdf

Workplace Gender Equality Agency (WGEA). (n.d.). *Superannuation & gender pay gaps by age group.* Australian Government. https://www.wgea.gov.au/publications/superannuation-gender-pay-gaps-by-age-group

Workplace Gender Equality Agency (WGEA). (2016). *Unpaid care and the labour market.* Australian Government. https://wgea.gov.au/sites/default/files/documents/australian-unpaid-care-work-and-the-labour-market.pdf

World Bank. (2023). *Gender data portal: Labor force participation (% of population).* https://genderdata.worldbank.org/en/indicator/sl-tlf-acti-zs?view=trend&geos=WLD

World Economic Forum. (2024). *Global gender gap report, 2024.* https://www3.weforum.org/docs/WEF_GGGR_2024.pdf

World Health Organization. (2024). *Violence against women.* https://www.who.int/news-room/fact-sheets/detail/violence-against-women

Xu, K. Q., & Payne, C. F. (2024). A growing divide: Trends in social inequalities in healthy longevity in Australia, 2001-20. *Population Studies, 78*(2), 231–250.

Yamamori, T. 2014. A feminist way to unconditional basic income: Claimants unions and women's liberation movements in 1970s Britain. *Basic Income Studies, 9*(1-2), 1–24.

Yamashita, J. 2017. A vision for post maternalism: institutionalising fathers' engagement with care. *Australian Feminist Studies, 31*(90), 432–447.

Yang, O., Yong, J., & Zhang, Y. (2024). Effects of private health insurance on waiting time in public hospitals. *Health Economics, 33*, 1192–1210.

Yap, M., & Biddle, N. (2012). *Unpaid work, unpaid care, unpaid assistance and volunteering* (CAEPR Indigenous Population Project, 2011 Census Paper 4). Centre for Aboriginal Economic Policy Research, ANU.

Yates, S., Carey, G., Hargrave, J., Malbon, E., & Green, C. (2021). Women's experiences of accessing individualised disability supports: Gender inequality and Australia's national disability insurance scheme. *International Journal for Equity in Health, 20*(243), 1–14.

Young, S. (2012). Childless? Adoption in Australia since the 1950s. *Island*, (129), 95–108.

Zelleke, A. (2008). Institutionalising the universal caretaker through a basic income? *Basic Income Studies: An International Journal of Basic Income Research, 3*(3), 1–9.

Zelleke, A. (2011). Feminist political theory and the argument for an unconditional BI. *Policy Politics, 39*, 27–42.

Appendices

Appendix 1—*detailed summary of research methodology*

Overall approach

The research conducted for this book drew on an interpretivist paradigm and was guided by a critical, intersectional feminist approach, which appreciates the patriarchal and other power dynamics that shape women's lives and opportunities, and which are compounded at the intersections of class, race, ability, and myriad other social characteristics (Crenshaw, 2017). Australian feminism of the mid-20th century was, in Aboriginal feminist and activist Pat Eatock's words, "predominantly middle class, educated and articulate" (Eatock, 1986 in Eatock & Eatock, 2003, p. 71). As Elizabeth Reid (2023, p. 23) later reflected in relation to her own experience of the Australian women's liberation movement, "Although we were sensitive to class, education, and articulateness, we failed to interrogate our very whiteness": an argument expertly articulated by Goenpul scholar and Distinguished Professor, Aileen Moreton-Robinson (2000). As a counterpoint to this history, the voices of Aboriginal and Torres Strait Islander women, migrant women, women belonging to different classes, with different abilities, and more, were intentionally sought in this research. To do so, a purposive sampling strategy (relying on recruitment via social media posts) was used to invite participants from across Australia, with an emphasis on achieving diversity. I describe the study sample in greater detail below. All participants were provided with honorariums in the form of untied gift cards to thank them for their time.

Scenario interviews

A qualitative "scenario interviewing" approach was adopted for this study. During the scenario interviews, women were presented with a UBI scenario for Australia and invited to imagine the potential implications of this for them, as well as for Australian women more broadly. Women were asked to focus on possible impacts around poverty reduction, economic security, autonomy, and freedom, though other topics and themes also arose organically, enabled by the semi-structured interview approach. The UBI scenario was the same for all women, involving a government-provided, taxable UBI set at $1,203 AUD per fortnight ($31,278 AUD per year)—that is, the Henderson poverty line for a single person at the March quarter, 2023 (see Melbourne Institute, 2023a, 2023b).

As discussed earlier, there is considerable variation in the levels of UBI proposed and/or piloted across the globe. The amount adopted for this study is, for example, slightly less than the proposed two-year UK trial of ~$1,516 AUD (£800) per fortnight (Ali Hussen, 2023), and slightly more than the Irish trial (from September 2022 to 2025) of ~$1,060 AUD (€650) per fortnight for artists (see Irish Government, 2022). In relation to UBI (or similar) proposals in Australia, this amount also sits at roughly the level set in the 2022 proposal by The Greens for a Liveable Income Guarantee (i.e., $88 AUD per day or $1,232 AUD per fortnight) (The Greens, 2022) and is slightly more than the amount proposed in the 2020 Liveable Income Guarantee (participation income) proposal by Quiggin et al. (2020a, 2020b), which used the aged pension as a benchmark (i.e., $944.30 AUD per fortnight at that time, or $1,002.50 AUD per fortnight using the 2023 rate). In keeping with the focus of this study on improving women's economic security, freedom, and autonomy, and also in line with the reasoning of others around the need for a UBI to enable poverty reduction, the Henderson poverty line was chosen as the most suitable benchmark for the UBI scenario in this research. (As I describe later in the findings section, when women were asked to nominate an amount prior to being told the scenario rate, their average response was only slightly higher.)

At the outset of each of the interviews, basic demographic data were collected, including age, average annual individual income, and more. Although income can provide an indication of the level of economic security experienced by women, it is not a perfect measure. Indeed, economic security itself as a concept is far broader, defined here as "the degree to which individuals are protected against hardship-causing economic losses" (Hacker et al., 2013, p. S7). This goes beyond, for instance, level of income, to also encompass assets/wealth, access to other avenues of economic support (e.g., via friends/family, public cash transfers, or other), and more (Kendall et al., 2019). For this reason, we used an economic security Likert scale, developed for this project, and pictured below (Figure 1A), during the interviews to get an approximate sense of women's subjective judgements of their own economic security. While validated economic security indexes and scales are available in the literature, these were not deemed suitable for the interview format used in this research (e.g., Hacker et al., 2013; Kendall et al., 2019;

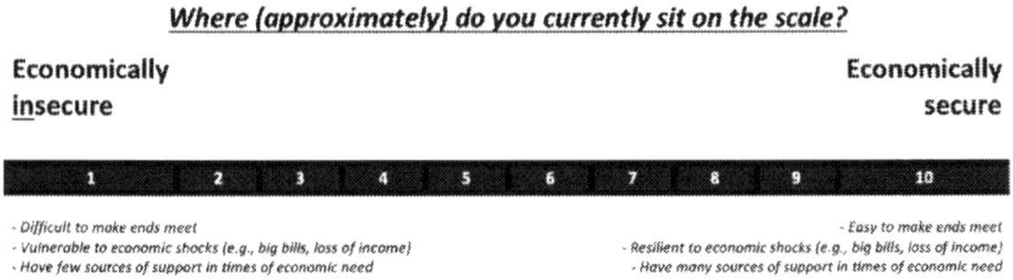

Figure 1A Economic security scale used during the interviews

Weller & Logan, 2009). Nevertheless, constructs and concepts used in other available indexes, such as economic volatility, adequacy, and wealth, were drawn upon and adapted for use in Figure 1A. This short Likert scale (Figure 1A) was visually shown and verbally explained to participants during the interviews before their responses were recorded. Each participant recorded two responses: (i) their position on the scale at the present time (when interviewed), *without* the hypothesised UBI, and (ii) their position on the scale *with* the hypothesised UBI.

Aside from two face-to-face interviews that were undertaken in Brisbane, the remaining 24 interviews were conducted via Zoom, as this allowed the study to draw on the perspectives of women from diverse geographic locations (i.e., far North, West, East, and South). The interviews took an average of 53 minutes each, ranging from ~30 minutes to 1 hour and 5 minutes. Twenty-four of the interviews were audio recorded and transcribed verbatim (with participants' consent), while one interview was recorded using written notes (as per the participant's wishes) and another was undertaken as a written interview conducted on email (also as per the participant's wishes). All participants were asked if they wished to receive their interview transcripts or notes so that they could make corrections or amendments prior to their inclusion in data analysis, with 16 (62%) taking up this option and two making suggestions for amendments that were then taken into the finalised transcripts. The finalised transcripts were analysed using NVivo software, adopting a mixed inductive and deductive thematic approach (Braun & Clarke, 2021), with deductive analysis identifying findings related to women's economic security, autonomy, and freedom. Some aspects of the interviews, which asked for quantitative data (e.g., around levels of economic security), were also compiled and descriptively analysed.

The project was conducted in accordance with ethical clearance received from The University of Queensland Human Research Ethics Committee (HREC) (2023/HE001058). All participants provided full, informed written consent to participate in the project and were also given the option to receive a summary and full report of the project findings (with most taking up this option).

Summary of study participants

All participants in this study identified as female. Other basic demographic details of the 26 participants for this study are outlined in Table 1A.

The sample had a median age of 36.5 years (min=20; max=63), which is slightly lower than the median age of all Australians (38 years) (ABS, 2021a, 2021b). Participants' incomes varied greatly (min=$10,000 per annum; max=$260,000 per annum), with the average sitting at $51,295.83: below the average annual income of Australian women overall (~$91,000) (ABS, 2023). There was also a very strong representation of women living with disability—70% of the total sample. This is far higher than the ~20% of all Australians who live with disability (AIHW, 2019). This coupling

Table 1A Basic demographic characteristics of the study participants

Demographic characteristics	*N (%)*
Age	
18–30	6 (22%)
31–43	11 (41%)
44–56	5 (19%)
57–69	4 (15%)
70+	0 (0%)
Total	***26 (100%)***
Indigenous status	
Identifies as Indigenous	3 (12%)
Does not identify as Indigenous	23 (88%)
Total	***26 (100%)***
Location	
Urban	20 (77%)
Non-urban	6 (23%)
Total	***26 (100%)***
Living with disability	
Yes	18 (70%)
No	8 (30%)
Total	***26 (100%)***
Employment status	
Employed (full time)	7 (27%)
Employed (part time)	11 (42%)
Not employed (working age)	8 (31%)
Retired	0 (0%)
Total	***26 (100%)***
Social security receipt	
Yes (one or more payments)	10 (38%)
No	16 (62%)
Total	***26 (100%)***

of disability and lower incomes is common in the broader population (PWDA, 2023), and some participants who experienced this told us this is what attracted them to participate in our study in the first place. That is, they already had an interest in UBI which was borne of their lived experiences as women living on lower incomes with often multiple care responsibilities, layered with their own needs for care and support.

Appendix 2—Australian Social expenditure (a)

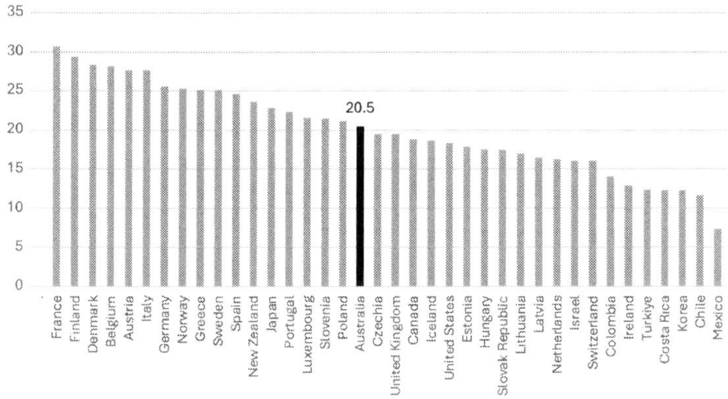

Figure 2A Australian overall social expenditure in 2019, as a total proportion (%) of gross domestic product (GDP)

Source: OECD (2024).

Appendix 3—Australian Social expenditure (b)

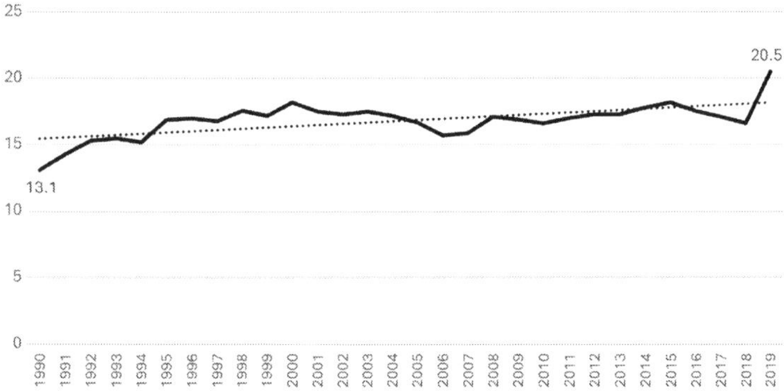

Figure 3A Australian overall social expenditure across time (1990–2019), as a total proportion (%) of gross domestic product (GDP)

Source: OECD (2024).

Appendix 4—proportion of female employees by industry type

Table 4A Proportion of female employees by industry type, 2018

Industry type	*Proportion (%) of female employees*	*Overall composition by sex*
Health care and social assistance	79%	Female-dominated
Education and training	73.2%	Female-dominated
Retail trade	55.0%	Mixed
Accommodation and food services	54.9%	Mixed
Administrative and support services	54.9%	Mixed
Public administration and safety	48.6%	Mixed
Rental, hiring, and real estate services	48.5%	Mixed
Financial and insurance services	48.1%	Mixed
Arts and recreation services	46.4%	Mixed
Other services	43.6%	Mixed
Professional, scientific, and technical services	43.3%	Mixed
Information media and telecommunications	42.0%	Mixed
Wholesale trade	34.7%	Male-dominated
Agriculture, forestry, and fishing	30.1%	Male-dominated
Manufacturing	29.5%	Male-dominated
Electricity, gas, water, and waste services	23.8%	Male-dominated
Transport, postal, and warehousing	20.9%	Male-dominated
Mining	16.3%	Male-dominated
Construction	12.0%	Male-dominated

Note: "Female-dominated" = 60% or more women; "Mixed" = 41%–59% women; "Male-dominated" = 40% or less women.

Source: WGEA (2019).

Appendix 5—remuneration by sex across female-dominated, male-dominated, and mixed industries

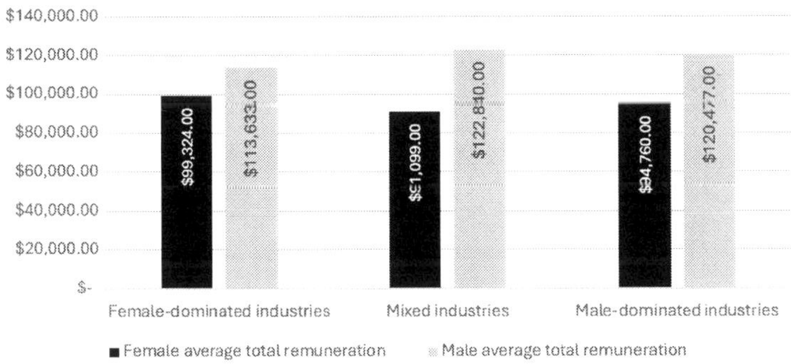

Figure 5A Average full-time total remuneration by female-dominated, mixed, and male-dominated industries (2018)

Note: "Female-dominated" = 60% or more women; "Mixed" = 41%–59% women; "Male-dominated" = 40% or less women.

Source: WGEA (2019).

Index

Made in the USA
Las Vegas, NV
19 September 2026

f937cf0a-8a1d-4fee-be12-7d256476d84bR01